CONTENTS

NOTE

In order to simplify the use of this book, all names, locations and geographic designations are as provided in *The Times World Atlas*, or other traditionally accepted major sources of reference, as of the time of described events. Similarly, Arabic names are romanised and transcripted rather than transliterated. For example: the definite article al- before words starting with 'sun letters' is given as pronounced instead of simply as al- (which is the usual practice for non-Arabic speakers in most English-language literature and media). For the reasons of space, ranges – which are usually measured in feet and nautical miles in international aeronautics – are cited in metric measurements only.

Helion & Company Limited
Unit 8 Amherst Business Centre, Budbrooke Road, Warwick CV34 5WE, England
Tel. 01926 499 619
Email: info@helion.co.uk   Website: www.helion.co.uk   Twitter: @helionbooks   Visit our blog http://blog.helion.co.uk/

Published by Helion & Company 2022
Designed and typeset by Farr out Publications, Wokingham, Berkshire
Cover designed by Paul Hewitt, Battlefield Design (www.battlefield-design.co.uk)

Text © Ali Altobchi with Tom Cooper & Adrien Fontanellaz 2022
Photographs © as individually credited
Colour artwork © Tom Cooper, David Bocquelet and Anderson Subtil 2022
Maps and diagrams © Tom Cooper 2022

ISBN 978-1-914377-18-1

British Library Cataloguing-in-Publication Data.
A catalogue record for this book is available from the British Library.

For details of other military history titles published by Helion & Company Limited contact the above address, or visit our website: http://www.helion.co.uk. We always welcome receiving book proposals from prospective authors.

ABBREVIATIONS

AAM	air-to-air missile
AB	air base
AEW	airborne early warning
AFB	Air Force Base
AOI	Arab Organization for Industrialisation
ASCC	Air Standardisation Coordinating Committee
AWACS	airborne early warning and control system
COMINT	communications intelligence
DIA	*Direction des Affaires Internationales* (Direction of International Affairs, part of the DMA, France)
DIA	Defense Intelligence Agency (USA)
DMA	*Délégation Ministérielle pour l'Armement* (Ministerial Delegation for Armament, France, 1965–1977)
ELINT	electronic intelligence
Flare	pyrotechnic device released from an aircraft causing an infrared homing missile or target tracker to follow it rather than the aircraft
GMID	General Military Intelligence Directorate (Iraq)
HAWK	Homing-All-The-Way-Killer (US-made SAM)
IAP	international airport
I-HAWK	Improved Homing-All-The-Way Killer (US-made SAM)
Il	Ilyushin (the design bureau led by Sergey Vladimirovich Ilyushin, also known as OKB-39)
IrAAC	Iraq Army Aviation Corps
IrAF	Iraq Air Force (official designation since 1958)
IRFNA	inhibited red fuming nitric acid (liquid rocket fuel)
IRGC	Islamic Revolutionary Guards Corps
IRIAF	Islamic Republic of Iran Air Force
KKMC	King Khalid Military City (Saudi Arabia)
MIC	Military Industrialization Commission (latter Directorate of Military Industries, Iraq)
MIMI	Ministry of Industry and Military Industrialisation (Iraq)
MiG	Mikoyan i Gurevich (the design bureau led by Artyom Ivanovich Mikoyan and Mikhail Iosifovich Gurevich, also known as OKB-155 or MMZ 'Zenit')
NATO	North Atlantic Treaty Organization
Raphael TH	*Radar de Photographie Aérienne Electronique á transmission hertzienne* (airborne-photography radar with electronic transmission)
RCC	Revolutionary Command Council
RDX	Research Department eXplosive
SAM	surface-to-air missile
SAMP	*Societe des Ateliers Mécaniques de Pont-sur-Sambre* (Company of the Mechanical Workshops of Pont-sur-Sambre)
SIGINT	signals intelligence
SSMD	Surface-to-Surface Missile Directorate (Iraq)
SSMRD	Surface-to-Surface Missile Research and Development (Committee, Iraq)
Su	Sukhoi (the design bureau led by Pavel Ossipovich Sukhoi, also known as OKB-51)
TNT	Trinitrotoluene
USSR	Union of Soviet Socialist Republics (also 'Soviet Union')

PREFACE

During the 1970s and early 1980s, and very slowly at first, Iraq grew an indigenous defence sector consisting of large factories, dozens of workshops, and multiple research facilities. Initially at least, the primary products included pistols, sub machine guns, assault rifles, machine guns, rocket-propelled grenades, and artillery ammunition. By the mid-1980s, the capability to manufacture tubes for artillery pieces, mortar ammunition, and aviation bombs up to 9,000kg was added. By the end of the same decade, the Iraqi defence sector was expanded to the degree where it bristled with research and development activity, and became capable of manufacturing intermediate range ballistic missiles, cruise missiles, unmanned aircraft, and of repurposing other weapons systems for new tasks.

Although thoroughly investigated by United Nations inspections between 1991–1995 – which resulted in a number of related publications – many details about the projects in question remain little-published upon, or at least unclear. Others remain entirely unknown. Naturally, the Western powers primarily paid attention to the Iraqi atomic-, biological-, and chemical weapons programmes which, by their sheer nature, represented the greatest threats. Therefore, these were the most carefully investigated. However, precise details about dozens of Iraqi armament factories and their products, as well as efforts to develop new weapons or modify existing ones, have largely evaded the public attention.

Based on a combination of the recollections of one of the engineers involved, and several writeups left by the late Brigadier General Ahmad Sadik Rushdie al-Astrabadi, an officer of the Intelligence Directorate of the Iraqi Air Force (IrAFID), the following study aims to correct at least some of that. It offers much new detail, a myriad of exclusive insights, recording and reminders of dozens of unknown projects, and enables a reinterpretation of several well-known but misunderstood, or intentionally misinterpreted, projects.

The reader is advised to keep in mind that the mass of Iraqi indigenous armament projects was conducted under conditions of the utmost secrecy and compartmentalisation for security purposes: everybody involved knew only as much as was necessary to accomplish his or her own task. In other cases, the sheer expansion of the projects in question was such that no single person could know everything. Finally, specific places in Iraq became notorious to the degree where – in a country with a national penchant for avoiding unpleasant facts – the Iraqis refuse to talk about them. Correspondingly, even those directly involved were frequently not in the possession of knowledge about all the details. In many other cases, they had only heard rumours. The situation has not improved due to the fact that because of the tragedies that have befallen Iraq since 1980, many of the participants have passed away, while others were scattered all over the world. Unsurprisingly, much related information remains obscure, or is irrecoverably lost. We do hope that the following account might help record at least the bare fundaments of the most important ideas, efforts and projects and prevent them from being forgotten.

1

FROM SOTI TO MIC

Knowing that Iraq was crafted by the British from the former Ottoman Wilayets of, from north to south, Mosul, Baghdad, and Basra in 1918–1931, an uniformed observer might expect the country to have never had its own defence industry at all. This impression is likely to be even greater considering the massive military build-ups through the import of major weapons systems – both from the West and the East – of the 1960s through to the 1980s. According to what is often published in the West, Mesopotamia – the ancient Greek name for the historical region of Western Asia situated within the Tigris-Euphrates river system – was almost void of human inhabitation and civilisation in 1910–1920. However, considering the involvement of a large number of highly-educated former Ottoman officers in the build-up of the Iraqi Army of the 1930s, this was not entirely true. Indeed, the local defence sector had a long – even if feeble – history.

Ammunition bunkers at the al-Qa'qaa complex – designed and built by Yugoslavia – shown in an aerial reconnaissance photograph from March 2003, released by the US Department of Defense. (US DoD)

FACTORIES 1, 2, AND AL-YARMOUK

It was back in the mid-1930s that the first two small factories for the production of pistols and – from the late 1930s – sub machine guns were constructed near al-Yusufiyah, south of Baghdad. Their capacity was very limited, and they remained unable to meet the needs of the constantly growing Iraqi Army, which thus remained dependent on imports of British- and Czechoslovak-made armament for the first 30 years of its existence. Indeed, thanks to British influence, very little changed in this regard until the Tammuz Revolution of 1958, when the new government of Brigadier General Abd al-Karim Qasim became the first to seriously consider a major expansion of the defence sector. However, the sole result of all the planning and efforts from this period was one facility: the al-Yarmouk Ammunition Factory. Located in Abu Garib, in western Baghdad, this produced small arms ammunition for the Iraqi Army. Continuous political turbulence, lack of funding and necessary know-how conspired against other plans, and it was only once the Ba'ath Party of Iraq established itself in power, in 1968, that the first steps in expanding the Iraqi armament industry were taken.

COOPERATION WITH YUGOSLAVIA AND THE AL-QA'QAA COMPLEX

In the course of two coups d'état staged in Baghdad on 17 July and 30 July 1968, an administration dominated by the Ba'ath Party established itself in power. The government that crystallised in the course of the second coup was named the Revolutionary Command Council (RCC) and was presided over by Major General Ahmed Hassan al-Bakr – a military officer. Contrary to the usual practice of earlier military governments of Iraq, Bakr, a popular military officer, was heavily dependent on the civilian wing of the Ba'ath for support: his cabinet included 26, foremost amongst whom was Saddam Hussein al-Mjid al-Tikriti. Originally in charge of the internal security of the party, and proven as a skilled organiser, by

November 1969 Saddam grew his reputation to the point where he was appointed the Vice-Chairman of the RCC, and thus Bakr's second in command. Bakr and Saddam were to form a duo that was to lead Iraq into an entirely new era.

Only months later, in early 1970, the RCC established the State Organisation for Technical Industries (SOTI), as a supreme planning and management body for the future defence sector. The importance of this project was already then considered high enough for the SOTI – while officially subordinated to the Ministry of Industry – to be presided over by nobody less than Saddam. Pursuing the idea of developing Iraq into the leading military power of the Arab world, he wasted no time in planning the construction of several arms factories, and research-, development-, and production facilities, all of which were – already at that point in time – intended to exceed the needs of the Iraqi armed forces. Such a vast and rapid expansion required many skilled workers and the kind of know-how rarely available in Iraq at that time. Therefore, Saddam sought foreign aid and advice. Always keen to apply the principle of balance between the East and the West, in 1972 he established links with Yugoslavia and quickly concluded a deal worth US$1 billion for the construction and delivery of two armament factories, and the education of thousands of Iraqi students in Yugoslavia.

In the same year, the construction of the al-Qaqaa State Establishment (also known as the Qa'qaa Explosives Factory) was launched by Yugoslav construction companies on a site between the towns of al-Yusufiyah and al-Iskandariya, relatively close to the former Factory No. 2, and 48km south of Baghdad. Nearby, the Huteen Artillery Ammunition Factory came into being, constructed in cooperation with the Union of Soviet Socialist Republics. Completed in 1980, the two factories were huge and employed thousands: 13,000 worked at al-Qa'qaa – which was of particular importance for the Iraqi armed forces, for it became capable of manufacturing Trinitrotoluene (TNT) and Research Department

Explosive (RDX) – and 10,000 at Huteen, which specialised in the production of artillery ammunition in calibres from 57mm to 152mm.

These first two projects were still under construction when, emboldened by their progress, Saddam contracted the Yugoslavs for more. Amongst these was the construction of Factory 72 for the production of explosives and ammunition, and the huge al-Qadessiya Factory, located next to the al-Qaqaa Complex. Both were in operation by 1980, by when al-Qadessiya launched the production of assault rifles of the AK-47 design, and RPG-7 rocket-propelled grenades.

Over the following years, the complex of Yugoslav-constructed state-owned armament factories continued growing. By 1986, the al-Qaqaa Complex covered an area of more than 28 square kilometres (nearly 11 square miles) and comprised 116 separate factories and workshops housed in more than 1,100 different structures. In addition to the al-Qaqaa Factory, the Huteen Artillery Ammunition Factory, Factories 2 and 72, and the al-Qadessiya Armament Factory, it included the Research and Development Centre, the Sumood Explosives Plant, and – later on – the Mustafa Missile Factory, Aqql Mamoun Missile Production Plant, the Latifiyah Phosgene and Solid Propellant Plant, Latifiyah Missile and Rocket Facility, Sulfuric Acid Plant, and Nitric Acid Plant, together with multiple static test stands.

COOPERATION WITH CZECHOSLOVAKIA

Initially at least, Yugoslavia was the most important partner for the Iraqi defence sector. However, the enormous extent of Saddam's planning surpassed the delivery capacities of just one country and – also because Czechoslovakia was keen to establish commercial links to oil-rich Iraq – the SOTI entered cooperation with the defence sector of Prague. In 1972, Czechoslovakia was contracted to establish an overhaul facility for OT-62 and OT-64 armoured personnel carriers that were meanwhile in the process of entering service with the Iraqi Army. The Czechoslovaks reacted by deploying two teams of six instructors each, and they helped install assembly jigs, tools, and testing equipment by late 1974. Because of a delay in construction works in Iraq, and the need to repair the related machinery after its long exposure to the local elements, the resulting factory was completed only in April 1976.

Understanding the need for the training of necessary personnel, in 1973 the Iraqi armed forces then hurried to establish the Military Technical College (MTC) in Baghdad. Developed with Czechoslovak assistance – despite the failure to secure the presence of 12 Czechoslovak teachers, as demanded by the Iraqis – the facility became fully operational in 1975–1976, and subsequently conducted active technical and scientific cooperation with Czechoslovak military institutions. By 1980, 15 Czechoslovak university professors were working at the MTC, while Iraqi researchers were trained in Brno in Czechoslovakia.

The Czechoslovak–Iraqi cooperation experienced a new boost in 1976, when – in response to an Iraqi request for involvement in further expansion of its defence sector – Prague submitted proposals for no less than four different factories. Amid fierce competition from numerous enterprises and governments, the SOTI distributed resulting contracts between Czechoslovakia, France, West Germany, the USSR and Yugoslavia: the Czechoslovak involvement resulted in a massive expansion of the al-Yarmouk Factory, and the construction of a plant for spherical powders, while the Yugoslavs were contracted with the construction of the al-Bakr Chemical complex for the production of explosives, largely equipped with machinery made in West Germany.

SOVIET INVOLVEMENT

Obviously, the successful involvement of Yugoslavia and Czechoslovakia brought the USSR into the plan. The Soviet Union was already in a sort of strategic partnership with Iraq since accepting a series of huge orders for arms between 1967 and 1970. In 1972, seeking for ways to free Iraq of Western influence, President Bakr – and his vice, Saddam Hussein – signed a 15-year friendship treaty with Moscow, which granted Iraq not only the acquisition of additional armament, but also Soviet support in further development of the recently nationalised Iraqi oil industry – an act that resulted in the doubling of Iraq's income from oil exports within just one year (a rate maintained for the rest of the decade).

That said, Moscow actually found itself uncertain how to handle Iraqi ambitions: the Soviet Union was already the primary arms supplier of Iraq, but relations with the RCC were anything but friendly, and thus the Kremlin saw its arms sales as a tool for influencing Baghdad's decision-making at the strategic level. On the other hand, while as keen to earn hard currency as anybody else, the Soviets lacked interest in helping the Iraqis developing domestic capacity: from their point of view, everything was fine as long as Iraq was buying arms, ammunition and equipment, and had it serviced in the USSR. Therefore, Moscow began meddling even in the negotiations with Czechoslovakia and Yugoslavia, and frequently making unrealistic offers at far more favourable conditions in order either to outbid the – nominally – 'allied' competition, or cause delays in the Iraqi decision-making and negotiations.

While such business methods functioned relatively well when it came to heavier weapons systems – primarily combat aircraft – they resulted in overly complex and costly arrangements, realised only with significant delays. For example, in May–June 1973, during trilateral negotiations between Iraq, Czechoslovakia, and the USSR, an agreement was reached for Czechoslovakia to construct a major military repair plant in Iraq. Under pressure from Moscow, the Iraqis agreed for the Soviets to provide the necessary technical documentation and advice. Obviously, they lacked both the tools and expertise in maintaining Czechoslovak-manufactured Aero L-29 Delfin training jets, and, despite the Iraqi wish for the resulting factory to be completed at the earliest possible date, this was finished only five years later in 1978. A similar fate befell the project for an aircraft repair facility. Originally planned to be developed in cooperation with Czechoslovakia, the facility – which reached its initial operational capability in 1975 – was eventually realised with Soviet support and was limited to undertaking repairs on L-29s. Due to the lack of specialised equipment, test devices, documentation, and trained personnel, it was only in 1979–1980 that it also became capable of undertaking complex overhauls on Soviet-made combat aircraft.

That the Soviets were only interested in pursuing their own interests became plain during the October 1973 Arab–Israeli War, and particularly during the Second Iraqi–Kurdish War of 1974–1975, when Moscow repeatedly refused to deliver the armament and equipment demanded by Baghdad, causing – amongst other things – severe shortages of specific types of ammunition. For example, while delivering 14 supersonic Tupolev Tu-22 bombers (ASCC/NATO codename 'Blinder') to the Iraqi Air Force (IrAF) in 1973, the Soviets delayed the delivery of bombs for them, resulting in the aircraft being effectively grounded during the war with Israel. A shipment of bombs arrived in time for the Tu-22s to see action

A Tupolev Tu-22 supersonic bomber of the Iraqi Air Force, taxiing at Taqaddum AB after returning from a strike on Mehrabad Air Base, in Tehran, late in the afternoon of 22 September 1980. (Tom Cooper collection)

against the Kurdish insurgents, but as soon as their armament – mainly the massive FAB-1500, FAB-3000, and FAB-9000 bombs – proved highly effective, Moscow refused to replenish Iraqi stocks.

The Soviet behaviour proved counterproductive before the end of the Second Iraqi–Kurdish War, because it prompted Saddam Hussein into several decisions. Starting in late 1974, he not only excluded Iraqi communists from the RCC, but launched their merciless persecution, leading to many becoming refugees in the USSR. Furthermore, he decided to diversify weapon acquisition in order to avoid dependence upon a single source. Finally, the experience reinforced his decision to build up a strong national military industry, capable of making the Iraqi armed forces autonomous. Always a good organiser, he understood that such a military industry required a skilled workforce. Supported by rapidly growing income from oil exports, in late 1974 he arrived at the decision to stipend the education of Iraqis willing to study abroad: over the following years, Baghdad thus paid for the education as engineers and technical specialists of at least 120,000 of its students, mainly in West Germany, Great Britain, and France. The condition was always the same: once back to Iraq, they were obliged to work in state-owned enterprises. Moreover, in an attempt to accelerate this process, the RCC established ties with the Arab Prospects and Development Organisation. With their help, the RCC reorganised and rapidly expanded all the technical schools and universities of Iraq, thus adding to the nation's capability to train a workforce necessary for its defence sector.

ALLIANCE WITH FRANCE

When searching for new customers for Iraq's oil, in 1972 Bakr and Saddam established links with Paris, and thus with the Ministerial Delegation for Armament (*Délégation Ministérielle pour l'Armement*, DMA): the top French authority for arms development. Established in the mid-1960s, the DMA had already proved highly influential in initiating the development of an entire new generation of French weapons systems. Starting in 1973, the its Direction of International Affairs (*Direction des Affaires Internationales*, DIA) began advertising the resulting products – foremost the Avions Marcel Dassault-Breguet Aviation (AMD-BA) Mirage F.1C interceptor. An offer of that kind came in handy for the Iraqis, who were about to find themselves confronted with Imperial Iran in the process of acquiring 80 of the brand-new and powerful, US-made Grumman F-14A Tomcat interceptors. However, the Iraqis were not satisfied with purchasing the aircraft 'off-the-shelf', as it was: on the contrary,

they demanded that the French develop the F.1C into a multi-role fighter-bomber, with equipment and armament that was advanced to the level where most of it was still on the drawing boards of the research and development departments of the companies involved. On top of that, they wanted to obtain the capability to maintain, repair, and overhaul the Mirages in Iraq, and to manufacture weapons for them. With such demands not only including the transfer of advanced know-how and high technology, but being extremely unusual at the time, the related negotiations went on for years, and it was only between November 1975 and July 1977 that a series of contracts was signed stipulating deliveries of 32 Mirage F.1EQ fighter-bombers, associated ground equipment, engines, and weaponry (Project Baz), and also 40 Aérospatiale SE.316C Alouette III helicopters armed with 264 AS.12 anti-tank guided missiles (ATGMs), 40 Aérospatiale SA.342 Gazelle helicopters armed with 360 advanced HOT ATGMs, nine Aérospatiale SA.321H and five SA.321GV Super Frelon helicopters armed with 60 of the latest Aérospatiale AM.39 Exocet sea-skimming anti-ship missiles. This was far from all: the contract for Project Baz included numerous sub-orders such as for 267 Matra Super 530F and 534 Matra R.550 Magic air-to-air missiles, Thomson-CSF TMV-002 Remora and Thomson-CSF TMV-004 Caiman electronic warfare pods, Thomson-CSF TMV-018 Syrel electronic intelligence pods, and Matra Sycomor chaff and flare dispensers. Another major order, Project Baz-AR, stipulated deliveries of a special version of the Matra AS.37 Martel anti-radiation missile, modified upon Iraqi request to such extent that it received a new designation, and including the option for licence production of it in Iraq. Notably, not one of all these weapons and electronic warfare systems were in production at the time that the related contracts were signed: on the contrary, most had yet to be developed sufficiently enough to enter series production and then be introduced to operational service. Indeed, in most cases this became possible solely thanks to Iraq's investment in them. On the negative side, all these complex processes took years to be completed, and even longer to reach Iraq. Nevertheless, the leadership in Baghdad was ready to accept such a delay, because – unlike the Soviets – the French were not only far more forthcoming in regards of delivering their 'best', but in regards of sharing the related know-how and maintenance facilities too.

ARAB ORGANISATION FOR INDUSTRIALISATION

Meanwhile, in 1975, the SOTI entered cooperation with the Arab Organization for Industrialisation (AOI) – a body based in Egypt,

A Nasser-9000 – the Egyptian-Iraqi copy of the massive, Soviet-designed FAB-9000M-54 bomb – on permanent display in front of the former HQ of the Iraqi Air Force, in Baghdad. (Photo by C.F. Foss)

Amer Rashid al-Obeidy shown in a photograph taken in 2000. (via Ali Tobchi)

Cairo thus gradually developed active cooperation with Czechoslovakia instead, which sold not only the know-how, but several factories for the production of ammunition and works capable of running periodic overhauls of Soviet-made combat aircraft, mainly the MiG-15, MiG-17, MiG-21, and Sukhoi Su-7. Production of munitions for fighter-bombers was lagging at first, but significantly bolstered during the early 1970s, when Egypt began manufacturing bombs of Soviet design, such as the FAB-50M-54, FAB-100M-54, FAB-250M-54 and FAB-250M-62, and FAB-500M-54 and FAB-500M-62. With Iraq in need of massive high-explosive bombs for its Tu-22 bombers, Baghdad and Cairo quickly found an agreement. The result was the Nasser-series of bombs – including Nasser-1500, Nasser-3000, Nasser-5000, and Nasser-9000, equivalent to FAB-1500M-54, -3000M-54, -5000M-54 and -9000M-54 – the casings for which were made in Egypt, and the explosives in Iraq. Arguably, their testing proved that the bombs delivered only about 60 percent of the overpressure created by the Soviet originals, but Baghdad was satisfied, for it was on the way to obtaining weapons necessary for the effective operation of its Tu-22 bombers.[1]

PROJECT SAAD-13: ELECTRONIC INDUSTRIES

The organisation of production of bombs for Tu-22s in cooperation with Egypt was just the first step in this direction. Displeased by a combination of repeated Soviet failures and refusals to deliver the armament demanded by Iraq, and well-financed thanks to the rapidly increasing oil wealth of the country, Saddam ordered Amer Rashid to find sources of new armament and technology transfers from the West, and this not only for purely military projects, but also for 'dual purpose' projects. For example, in 1978, an iron and steel-works constructed by the French company Creusot-Loire was opened at Qowr az-Zubayr, which produced smelted iron ore and steel. Certainly enough, the Soviets were still granted some contracts – such as for the construction of a tractor factory in al-Musayyib, opened in 1978 – but generally, that was a 'drop on the hot rock' in comparison to additional contracts with Western companies.

No other project related to the Iraqi indigenous armament industry of the late 1970s was as important and far-reaching as the one initiated by Amer Rashid in 1978: encouraged by the successful conclusion of the contracts for projects Baz and Baz-AR, he was obsessed with the idea of developing electronic industries in Iraq. Correspondingly, during the second half of that year he opened a contest for the construction of a factory to produce radio sets and radars. Amid fierce competition between the British company Plessey and the French Thomson-CSF, Amir Rahid skilfully negotiated a favourable contract with the French. Thus came into being Project Saad-13, worth FF4 billion (about US$900 million at the time), signed in 1980.

but sponsored by Kuwait, Saudi Arabia, and United Arab Emirates, aiming to collectively develop an Arab arms industry. Saddam appointed Amer Mohammed Rashid al-Obeidy (colloquially 'Amer Rashid') as a head of the AOI in Iraq, a young and gifted electronics-engineer, determined to develop domestic electronic industry as a key to all the modern weapons systems. To underline Rashid's status and stress his position vis-à-vis the regular Iraqi armed forces, he was – just like Saddam and the new Minister of Defence, Adnan Khairallah – assigned the honorary rank of a general.

Sadly, bitter rivalry between the governments involved in the AOI – many of which feared an Iraqi dominance – prevented most of the plans from being realised. Nevertheless, the existence of this umbrella organisation did help bolster cooperation between Baghdad and Cairo, resulting in the production of infantry arms and ammunition, and of aviation bombs. Following its split with the USSR, between 1972 and 1976, Egypt found itself in possession of a large arsenal of Soviet-made armament: however, the Soviets were always reluctant to deliver the necessary support infrastructure.

A sad recollection of better times: one of 86 GCT-155 howitzers acquired by Iraq in the late 1970s, seen after its capture by US troops in 2003. (US DoD)

Project Saad-13 was kept secret to the degree that it was never officially announced – whether in Iraq or in France – although several hundreds of French architects and engineers were deployed in Iraq, and more than 3,000 Iraqi students travelled to France for related education. The most talented amongst the latter were selected for specialised education at a new training centre set up by Thomson-CSF just for this purpose. During the first half of the 1980s, Project Saad-13 resulted in the construction of a complex of major industrial facilities near Saddam's birthplace in ad-Dour village, near the town of Tikrit, 140km north of Baghdad. There, supervised by French architects and engineers, factories for the production of integrated circuits and quartz crystals for radios came into being, with the aim of, later on, becoming capable of manufacturing radars, and becoming involved in various sub-projects of Baz.

Unsurprisingly, when the DIA made an offer of GCT-155 self-propelled howitzers to Iraq, it attracted attention in Baghdad. Theoretically, acquisition of such systems was another critical issue for the Iraqi armed forces, because during the mid- and late 1970s, both Iran and Israel were acquiring hundreds of US-made M109 self-propelled howitzers, capable of firing 155mm shells out to a range of 21,000m. Eventually, in a deal arranged via the AOI, Iraq did acquire 86 GCT-155s (concurrently with a Saudi order for 63 units), but had the chassis heavily modified after finding it unsuitable for operations in desert conditions. However, the further acquisition of GCT-155s was then stopped in favour of an even more advanced weapon, about which more is to follow in a subsequent chapter.

Successful negotiations for Project Saad-13 encouraged Amer Rashid to convince Saddam to further intensify such efforts and open a contest for the construction of an aircraft overhaul facility. Much to Amer Rashid's disappointment, this project was cancelled shortly after the outbreak of the war with Iran in September 1980. Nevertheless, he remained convinced that the longer it took to develop Iraq's own defence sector, the more the country would be forced to continue purchasing from abroad. Therefore, he was not frustrated by this experience but it only reinforced his efforts: negotiations for the construction of an aircraft overhaul facility were renewed with both Great Britain and France several times during the 1980s.

Massive Iraqi orders for French weapons caused an outburst of protests from Moscow, which began exercising pressure upon Baghdad. While Saddam was unimpressed, during the last years of his tenure Bakr did attempt to appease the Soviets and thus the SOTI contracted the Soviets for several projects. These included what became the Saddam Factory in Falluja, which launched licence production of Soviet-designed D-30 122mm howitzers; the ash-Shaheed Factory, which manufactured copper cases for artillery shells; the ad-Dor Factory (also known as Salahuddin Works; 120km north of Baghdad) for production of wireless devices and included the al-Ba'ath Institute for training the necessary workforce; and a tractor factory. All of these facilities became operational through the first half of the 1980s. In combination, the indigenous Iraqi arms industry thus became capable of producing ammunition from 5.56mm to 130mm calibre, pistols, sub machine guns, hand grenades, mortar bombs and ammunition for RPG-7s, followed by artillery pieces, wireless sets and radars, together with associated tools and other equipment.

MILITARY INDUSTRY COMMISSION

Despite the rapid growth of the indigenous arms industry, the spate of major arms deals and orders for construction of armament factories from the mid-1970s all came much too late to make Iraq independent in this field before the outbreak of the war with Iran in September 1980. Similarly, regardless of how massive, efforts to upgrade industrial capacity from the extraction and processing of natural resources to heavy industry, and the manufacturing of higher technology and the production of consumer goods, fell short of the plan: Iraq could not acquire and assimilate the necessary know-how and industrial capacity at the pace desired by Saddam and Ahmed Rashid. Another major issue was organisational by nature, resulting in a very unusual condition in the defence sector. Although the RCC engaged in extensive central planning, it largely concentrated on management of natural resources and foreign trade, while leaving most of the industry, services, and agriculture to private enterprise. In similar fashion, the SOTI was preoccupied with the establishment of the first few factories to a degree where it had no capacity to deal with the acquisition and construction of additional facilities. Considering Iraq's oil wealth, the RCC's preoccupation with exploitation and export of natural resources was little surprising: after all, this provided about 95 percent of foreign exchange earnings, in turn financing the industrial development. However, this resulted in a situation where up to 67 percent of about 700 industrial establishments in existence as of 1980 were privately owned, and they were turning out about 40 percent of the total industrial production, but the mass of them were actually small workshops, rarely employing more than 20 or 30 workers. On the contrary, major enterprises were all state-owned, and out of a total industrial labour force of about 150,000, 80 percent were working for state-owned companies.

This is why Saddam found himself under severe pressure once, following the outbreak of the war with Iran, the USSR imposed an arms embargo, and all of its allies in Eastern Europe followed in fashion. Suddenly, Iraq – whose armed forces were still largely equipped with Soviet-designed weapons systems – found itself facing a critical shortage of most ammunition types and spare parts, and in a dire need to replace any piece of heavy equipment lost in combat. Several Iraqi delegations travelled abroad to secure urgent deliveries: regardless if in the East or the West, most found themselves facing indifference, if not an outright refusal. Only Italy and Egypt proved keen to intensify cooperation. Eventually, Saddam Hussein found no other solution than to further intensify the development of the indigenous defence sector. For this purpose, he reorganised the SOTI into the Military Industry Commission (MIC). Subordinated to the Ministry of Industry and Minerals, it concentrated on controlling all the companies already involved in the manufacture of explosives, firearms, guns, rockets, and mortar bombs, and reconfiguring several other factories for similar purposes.

The importance of the MIC was best demonstrated by the fact that right from the start it was under the control of two of Saddam's closest confidantes: in addition to Amer Rashid, the second was Hussein Kamil Hassan al-Majid (colloquially, 'Hussein Kamil'). They received the very clear task of expanding the national defence industry sector to minimise dependence upon – and vulnerability to – external factors, but also to be a leading edge for military training and the development of skills for the civilian sector, and to lower foreign exchange expenditure and dependence. Hussein Kamil and Amer Rasheed quickly established the MIC as a dominant force within the AOI, the structure of which was used to widen cooperation with the Egyptian defence sector, from which Iraq had meanwhile been importing the mass of its infantry arms and ammunition. In turn, through cooperation with Egypt, the Iraqis became capable of using the AOI as a front for placing orders for advanced weaponry elsewhere, and thus avoiding a variety of arms embargos imposed upon Baghdad, or at least evading the arms export laws of most of the Western powers.

The net result was ironic: while the MIC excelled in growing a large network of front companies abroad and securing further orders for large amounts of military equipment, the growth of capability to manufacture armament at home remained slow. That said, from that period onwards, every single arms deal was accompanied with a sub-contract for the transfer of know-how and technology, often enough for a full transfer of production facilities. Combined with the return of thousands of Iraqi engineers and specialists from training abroad, this was to result in the emergence of numerous research centres and factories capable of manufacturing dual-use goods: goods for both civilian and military purposes over the next few years.

2
WAR WITH IRAN

Following months of mass popular protests and strikes all over the country, in February 1979 Shah Reza Pahlavi of Iran was toppled in what subsequently became known as the 'Islamic Revolution'. Relations between that country and Iraq – regulated by the Algiers Treaty of 1975 – worsened over the following months, reaching a point where both governments began supporting armed opposition against the other, and even launching assassination attempts against top diplomats. With the new Iranian government publicly threatening to 'export' its Islamic Revolution to Iraq, by August 1980 the crisis reached a point where a series of bitter border skirmishes erupted. Knowing that the Iranian armed forces were in complete disorder due to the post-revolutionary chaos, Saddam convinced himself and the rest of the RCC that this was not only the opportunity to invade, but also to pre-empt an Iranian invasion of Iraq. Thus, on 22 September 1980, Iraq opened the war with air strikes on nearly two dozen air bases, airfields and other military facilities in Iran, followed by an onslaught of its mechanised forces into the oil-rich province of Khuzestan, all – nominally – with the aim of securing the Shatt al-Arab waterway and driving Iranian artillery beyond the range of the nearest Iraqi urban centres.

Although encountering surprisingly bitter Iranian resistance and advancing very slowly, by the end of October 1980 the Iraqis were in the outskirts of Dezful and surrounded the port of Khorramshahr: while the garrison of the former held, that of the latter was eventually overrun, marking the high tide of the Iraqi invasion. However, in the meantime, the Islamic Republic of Iran Air Force (IRIAF) not only recovered from the shock it experienced at the start of the war but hit the Iraqi oil industry so severely that it had not recovered even nine years later. Combined with the onset of the rain season, and murderous IRIAF air strikes on the Iraqi Army formations exposed in the open and flat terrain of western Khuzestan, this made any further advance impossible. By early 1981, the war settled into a terrible routine: several times a year, the Iranians would unleash massive concentrations of their ground forces into offensives against Iraq. Operations conducted through 1981 and early 1982 aimed to liberate parts of Khuzestan, but from mid-1982, and for the next five years, Iran repeatedly tried to capture Basra, the second-largest city in Iraq, or break the back of the Iraqi armed forces through cutting Basra from Baghdad.

WEAPON OF DETERRENT

The RCC originally expected the war to be over in a matter of weeks – if not days – and the government in Tehran to either capitulate or be toppled by a more acceptable party. Thus, the longer the conflict went on, the more concerns it caused in Baghdad, imposing ever new priorities not only for the government. By early 1981, Saddam Hussein, Hussein Kamil, and Amer Rashid all concluded that Iraq needed a 'weapon of deterrent': a system capable of striking deep into Iran in the way the IRIAF was striking Iraq, with the aim of delivering blows upon the enemy's morale and thus forcing Tehran into a negotiated ceasefire. This became plainly obvious in 1982 when, although Saddam ordered a general withdrawal of the Iraqi armed forces back to the internationally recognised border, the Iranian leaders remained intransigent. They insisted on continuing the war in the form of an invasion of Iraq even once Saudi Arabia offered to pay for the damage caused by the conflict up to that point in time, and despite unreasonably high losses to their armed forces.

PROJECT 84

While studying the condition of Iraq's arsenal, the leadership in Baghdad concluded that the available systems were insufficient. Older bombers like the Tupolev Tu-16 and Tu-22 did fly deep into Iranian airspace early during the war but proved vulnerable to enemy air defences and suffered unacceptably high losses. By 1982, the Iraqi Air Force (IrAF) had five Soviet-made MiG-25RB reconnaissance/ strike-fighters (ASCC/NATO codename 'Foxbat B') in service with the newly established No. 87 Squadron. The introduction to service of this type with the IrAF was conducted under the codename Project 84. Capable of accelerating up to Mach 2.83 while operating at altitudes above 21,000m (69,000ft), Foxbat easily avoided all the Iranian air defences. However, while equipped with the Peleng-D navigation/attack system that enabled them to aim bombs, Iraqi examples were never equipped with bomb shackles and special, insulated FAB-500T bombs to arm them (insulation was necessary to reduce the heat caused by air friction at high speeds): Moscow refused to deliver these.[1] Therefore, it appeared that MiG-25RBs could not be deployed as Iraq's weapon of deterrent. Similar was true for what was to become the 'star' of the Iraqi Air Force during this conflict: ordered in 1977, the French-made Dassault Mirage F.1EQ jets were now in the process of delivery, but initially available as interceptors only: deliveries of their multi-role (or 'fighter-bomber') sub-variants were to start only in 1985. Moreover, they had a

relatively short range, and would become capable of striking targets deep inside Iran only with the help of in-flight refuelling (IFR) operations. The latter were not only extremely risky, but to become possible only once France started delivering the Mirage F.1EQ-4 variant, equipped with the necessary IFR probes, in 1984.

THE FIRST IRAQI BALLISTIC MISSILES

Another weapon with a longer range in the Iraqi arsenal was the ballistic missile. Iraq began acquiring such systems from the USSR in 1972, when Moscow agreed to sell 9K52 Luna-9M rocket systems (ASCC/NATO codename 'FROG-7'). Fired from the 9P113 transporter-erector-launcher (TEL), its spin-stabilised 9M21 rockets could deliver a 420–457kg warhead over a range of only 70km, with a circular error probability (CEP) of about 400 metres. FROGs entered service with Missile Brigade 225 in 1975. The latter included two firing units (Battalions 135 and 136), a headquarters section, and a meteorological section, equipped with a total of four TELs and manned by 180 officers and other ranks.

Four 9P113 TELs of Missile Brigade 223, Iraqi Army, seen during a military parade in Baghdad in the late 1970s. (Author's collection)

Another view of the same four vehicles, showing details of their camouflage pattern and the missiles carried. (Author's collection)

ENTER THE SCUD

Obviously, the Luna-9M lacked the range to strike deep into Iran. Thus, only two years after acquiring these, and in the light of Egyptian and Syrian experiences from the October 1973 Arab–Israeli War, Baghdad requested delivery of the longer-ranged R-17E ballistic missile (ASCC/ NATO codename 'SS-1c Scud-B'). A follow-up to the earlier R-11, the R-17E entered service with the Soviet armed forces in 1964. It was a relatively crude, liquid-fuelled missile with a primitive inertial guidance system centred on a gyroscope. The guidance system controlled the movement of vane type jet deflectors positioned in the exhaust of a liquid-propellant motor but guided the weapon only during the first – powered – phase of flight: once the motor was shut down, the entire missile – including the warhead – coasted unguided to the target. It was notorious for its poor accuracy and was ever more inaccurate the further it flew. The 5,900kg (when fully fuelled) R-17E had a range of 270–300km. Surprisingly enough, as of 1974 Moscow quickly agreed to deliver 40 R-17E missiles and six 9P117 TELs (better known as 'MAZ-543' in Iraq), and to provide training for their crews. Scuds thus became operational with Missile Brigade 224 of the Iraqi Army in 1976. By 1980, the number of imported R-17Es increased to 112, and by 1988, Baghdad was to purchase a total of 819 R-17E missiles and ten MAZ-543 TELs from the USSR.

Missile Brigade 224 was involved in the war against Iran right from the start. On 22 September 1980, it targeted Tactical Fighter Base 4 (TFB.4), outside the town of Dezful, with six R-17Es, and the nearby Andimeshk Highway Strip with another three missiles. On 7 October 1980, Missile Brigade 224 fired its third volley of the war, when three R-17Es were launched at TFB.4. According to the Iranians, all of these missiles missed, but the last three hit the town of Dezful, causing over 270 civilian casualties. Later in October 1980, the unit fired several R-17Es at TFB.2, outside Tabriz in north-western Iran, and at TFB.3 near Hamedan – all with unknown results.[2]

As soon as Moscow lifted the arms embargo in March 1981, the MIC requested delivery of additional Scuds, and also longer-ranged missiles like the 9M76/TR-1 Temp (ASCC/NATO codename 'SS-12 Scaleboard'), with a range of 800km. While agreeing to sell more of R-17Es, the Soviets flatly refused to provide any kind of longer-ranged weaponry to Iraq. Baghdad was thus left without a choice but to search for its weapon of deterrent somewhere else.

OTR-1 Temp ('SS-12 Scaleboard') system of the Soviet Army, as requested by Iraq in 1981. Its general appearance was quite similar to that of the SS-1 Scud: it used the same MAZ-543 TEL, but the 9,700kg missile was shrouded into a protective container which served as a launcher. (US DoD)

3

FRENCH AND SOVIET ANTI-RADIATION MISSILES

As described in Chapter 1, the Iraqi order for Mirage F.1EQ fighter-bombers from November 1975 – July 1977 stipulated not only the deliveries of the jets and directly related equipment, but the development of an entire range of electronic warfare systems. One of the most important of these was the Baz-AR anti-radiation missile, the deliveries of which resulted in an 'arms race' between France and the Soviet Union.[1]

MAGICS FOR MiGS

As so often when it comes to such complex weapons systems, the first arms to reach Iraq under Project Baz were air-to-air weapons. Amongst these were Matra R.550 Magic (later: Magic Mk.I) short-range, infrared homing air-to-air missiles. At the time, the Magic was still a brand-new weapon: it reached its initial operational capability in 1975, but even if the production at Salbris was ramped up to the rate of about 100 per month, it was still not in widespread use even in France. Magic was very agile and had a very wide engagement envelope: it could acquire targets flying 140° off boresight and had one of the shortest minimum engagement ranges amongst contemporary air-to-air missiles: a mere 300 metres. The first batch arrived in Iraq during the summer of 1980 and – because the construction of the custom-tailored base for Mirages, the future Saddam AB, was still incomplete – was initially stored at Hurrya AB outside Kirkuk. This is how it came to be that the French missiles were 'inspected' by technicians of No. 47 Squadron, a brand-new unit that was in the process of completing its training on recently delivered MiG-21bis interceptors. Soon, the Iraqis concluded that the R.550 was interchangeable with the Soviet-made R-13M short-range, infrared homing missile (ASCC/NATO codename 'AA-2D Atoll') and had its seeker head cooled in similar fashion: by liquid nitrogen from a bottle installed in the launch rail. The reason was that just as the earlier Soviet R-3S ('AA-2A Atoll') air-to-air missile was a copy of the US-made AIM-9B Sidewinder, the R-13M was a copy of the more advanced AIM-9D Sidewinder, and the French – wisely – aimed to make their missile easy to adapt to US-made aircraft in order to attract more export orders. As a result, the MiG-21bis of No. 47 Squadron were regularly armed with French-made R.550 Magic air-to-air missiles, and this practice was continued well into the 1980s.

A prototype of the Baz-AR installed on the centreline pylon of a Mirage F.1EQ-2 (serial number 4004) during testing in France. (Dassault, via Michel Benichou)

PROJECT BAZ-AR

Meanwhile, the French company Matra was working on developing the anti-radiation missile ordered by Iraq in 1976. With the Baz-AR being based on the Matra/Hawker Siddeley Dynamics AJ.168/AS.37 Martel anti-radiation missile, its development advanced quite quickly. The French took care to replace all the components of British and US origin with their own technology. The latter included an entirely new, broad-band passive seeker designated ADAR ('*autodirector anti-radiation*') that could not only be pre-set to search for a specific frequency before the take-off, but also adjusted by the pilot once the aircraft was airborne. Although much underestimated to the present day – mainly because it was overshadowed by contemporary US and Soviet progress in the same field – work on the Baz-AR also resulted in a missile with an exceptional range and a deadly warhead (largest in the world for any anti-radiation missile).[2]

Flight testing was initiated in France in February 1980, and the first powered test flight in November of the same year: the first telemetry test of the Baz-AR – using a missile with a live seeker head but without a warhead – took place on 21 April 1981 and was concluded successfully. Following additional refining and two additional test-firings, the weapon was declared operational in November 1981, and the first shipment of 30 reached Iraq by the end of the same year, followed by another (of 30 rounds) in 1982.

THE SOVIET CHALLENGE

The first four Mirage F.1EQ-2s were delivered to Iraq in late January 1981. They were followed by the second transfer, in early March of the same year. In Iraq, they were based at the newly constructed Saddam Air Base, north of Tikrit, and operated by No. 79 Squadron, Iraqi Air Force, which initiated its operations in September 1981. By the end of the year, they claimed several aerial victories against Grumman F-14 Tomcat interceptors and McDonnell Douglas F-4 Phantom II fighter-bombers of the IRIAF. However, their deliveries, and those of related equipment, still occurred rather slowly, and – five years after its order – the Baz-AR missile was still not in service with the IrAF.

A dusty Kh-28 ('AS-9 Kyle') anti-radiation missile (left, foreground) next to an Iraqi Su-22M-2K, captured by US Army troops at Ali Ibn Abu Talib AB in March 1991. (US DoD)

Another view of the same jet, with the Kh-28 near the wall, still on its trolley. The missile included a 140kg 9A283 warhead equipped with a ROV-5 proximity fuse. The large fuel and oxidiser tanks occupied the centre fuselage, with the APR-28 autopilot positioned in between of fuel tanks and the R-253-300 engine. (US DoD)

Meanwhile, only days after the transfer of the second batch of Mirage F.1EQ-2s to Iraq, and after months of intensive efforts to court Tehran ended nowhere, the leadership in Moscow had second thoughts and decided to lift its arms embargo imposed upon Iraq. In May 1981, deliveries of Soviet armament ordered before 22 September 1980 were resumed. Indeed, by this time the USSR was keen to recover its prestige in Baghdad and thus went as far as to send six KKR-1TE/2MK reconnaissance pods, associated equipment, and a team of specialists to Firnas AB, outside Mosul, to convert four Su-22Ms of No. 5 Squadron into reconnaissance fighters. Two additional

Soviet teams followed in quick succession: one helped the Iraqis to make operational their MiG-23MF interceptors while the other did the same with MiG-25RB reconnaissance-strike jets and MiG-25PU conversion trainers: both types were delivered to Iraq in the summer of 1980, but due to the Soviet embargo – and the resulting lack of documentation and support equipment – were never pressed into service. As a result, No. 67 Squadron was declared operational on MiG-23MFs and No. 87 Squadron on MiG-25s – both by the end of 1981. The race to deliver more advanced weapons to Iraq was now open.

The wreckage of another Su-22M-2K of the IrAF found by US Army troops inside another hardened aircraft shelter at Ali Ibn Abu Talib AB. Clearly visible in the centre – still installed on the inboard underwing hardpoint – is the Myetel targeting pod, necessary for target acquisition for the Kh-28. (US DoD)

One of the few Kh-28s left in Iraq after the end of the war in Iran – found by US troops in 2003 still stored inside its transportation container. The Kh-28 proved a powerful but cumbersome weapon, largely due to its liquid fuel – a similar, highly toxic and corrosive mix of inhibited red fuming nitric acid oxidiser (IRFNA) and kerosene to that used on Soviet-made R-17E ballistic missiles (ASCC/NATO codename 'SS-1b Scud-C'). This meant that it had to be fuelled and defueled before and after every operational sortie. (US DoD)

In autumn 1981, the Soviets went a step further and delivered a batch each of Kh-28C and Kh-28E (ASCC/NATO codename 'AS-9 Kyle') anti-radiation missiles and associated Myetel guidance pods necessary for their deployment. The Kh-28 represented 'the best' of Soviet technologies of the 1960s. It was a scaled-down version of Raduga's (much larger) Kh-22 anti-ship missile (ASCC/NATO codename 'AS-4 Kitchen'), usually carried by modified Tu-22K bombers. However, at nearly six metres in length, and with a launch weight of 715kg (140kg of which was the warhead), it was still a hefty load for a tactical aircraft – even more so considering its deployment required the same jet to also carry the Myetel targeting pod. Kh-28s and Myetels arrived together with another team of technicians that helped upgrade four or five Su-22Ms of the Firnas-based No. 5 Squadron to the standard locally known as 'Su-22M-2K'. The Soviet military attachés in Baghdad then encouraged the IrAF to deploy these in combat against Iranian MIM-23Bs. The modified Su-22M-2Ks flew their first operational sortie on 27 October 1981: although one was shot down by an F-14A, and the rest of the formation released its missiles from the maximum range of 70km, their strike took the Iranians by surprise and resulted in the confirmed destruction of six high-power illuminator (Doppler) radars of the I-HAWKs. For the first time in the history of aerial warfare in the Middle East, an 'Arab' air force was in possession of a weapon clearly outmatching its opponent.

The successful deployment of Kh-28s put the French under immense pressure – even more so because the first two test-firings of the Baz-AR in Iraq both ended in failure. In May 1982, Paris recalled the entire stockpile of missiles back to France for detailed inspection and an additional test launch. The result was a manual providing detailed instructions on how to operate the weapon, including advice to power it up at least five minutes before release. Nevertheless, the next Iraqi test-firing – undertaken on 6 August 1982 – was unsuccessful yet again. Now the gloves were off: the French set up a special team including Dassault and Matra's project managers, electronic specialists and test-pilots of the French air force. Conducted in October 1982, their tests were all concluded successfully, and the weapon officially declared operational: on 25 December 1982, four Mirage F.1EQ-2s from No. 79 Squadron flew their first operational sortie against Iranian MIM-23Bs, and, reportedly, scored four hits. Project Baz-AR was thus saved from cancellation. However, contrary to original Iraqi intentions, no technology-transfer ever took place, and the IrAF never went beyond acquiring between 60 and 80 missiles. Exactly how many of these were deployed in combat remains unknown. In comparison, it is known that between 1981 and 1983, it received a total of 115 Kh-28s from the USSR, of which no

A Kh-28 painted in white overall, with a large Iraqi flag on its fin, on display during the May 1989 arms fair in Baghdad. At the time, the Iraqis claimed to have launched licence production of this weapon though no such project was ever realised. (Photo by Peter Foster)

fewer than 104 were fired in combat by 1988. That said, just like in the case of the Baz-AR, due to the astronomic costs of fighting the war with Iran, even this project did not go as far as some Iraqis wanted: contrary to claims published by official Iraqi representatives later on, even if receiving the local designation Nissin-28, the Kh-28 was never manufactured in Iraq under licence.

IN-FLIGHT REFUELLING

As of the 1960s–1980s, in a world still dominated by racism, it was next to unheard of for customers outside the USA or Europe to demand that arms manufacturers redesign their weapons to their own requirements. The first to change its stance vis-à-vis such requests was Dassault when, in the early 1960s, it met the Israeli demand to install two 30mm DEFA guns in its brand-new, rocket-assisted, high-altitude, radar-equipped and missile-armed Mirage IIIC interceptor. Over the following years, Dassault went as far as to follow additional Israeli requirements and adapt the same design to one for a fighter-bomber without radar, specialised in low-altitude operations. Thus came into being the Mirage 5, which Iraq ordered in 1968, only for the related contract to be cancelled in mutual agreement between Baghdad and Paris a few months later, amid severe pressure from the left-wing circles in France. As described above, even once Iraq eventually placed its order for Mirage F.1 interceptors, nearly a decade later, it still insisted on this design being modified from another high-altitude, missile-armed interceptor, into a fighter-bomber that was to excel in low-altitude operations. Moreover, Iraqi orders resulted in the emergence of a number of high-technology weapons systems custom tailored to Iraqi requirements – the research and development of which was financed by Baghdad, too.

Two F.1EQ-4s in the process of in-flight refuelling training from an Il-76MD transport modified to serve as a tanker in 1983. This solution was concluded to be impracticable. (via Ali Tobchi)

Eventually, the French modified the Mirage F.1EQ-4 with the capability to carry the Douglas/Intertechnique D-704 in-flight refuelling pod under the centreline, thus providing a 'tanker' aircraft enabling Iraqi Mirage F.1EQ-4s and F.1EQ-5s to strike targets deep inside Iran. This photograph was taken in 1985, during one of many related training sorties. (via Ali Tobchi)

By 1989, the Iraqis had rebuilt the first Il-76 transport used for testing in-flight refuelling, and this was demonstratively flown over Baghdad during a military parade in 1990, accompanied by two Mirage F.1EQ-4s or F.1EQ-5s. (Tom Cooper collection)

By 1981, the Mirage F.1EQ-2 was in operational service in Iraq, and Baghdad demanded their further improvement. One of the new requirements was for the jet to receive an in-flight refuelling capability in order to be able to reach Tehran. In February 1982, this resulted in the order for the sub-variant designated Mirage F.1EQ-4, equipped with an in-flight refuelling probe. However, the acquisition of F.1EQ-4s – deliveries of which were scheduled to start in 1983 (and to last through mid-1984) – was only half the solution: now the IrAF needed an aircraft that could supply its future Mirages with fuel in the air. Lacking anything similar, the Iraqis improvised at first: a Soviet-made fuel truck was parked and secured inside the cargo hold of an Ilyushin Il-76MD transport and connected to a Douglas/Intertechnique D-704 refuelling pod installed underneath the rear cargo door of the big jet. This solution was soon discarded: the relatively short range of the Mirage meant that in order to reach targets as far as Tehran the in-

A mural showing a Tu-16-bomber modified through the installation of D-704 pods, providing fuel to two Mirage F.1EQs, as flight tested in 1989. (via Ahmad Sadik)

flight refuelling part of the mission would have to be undertaken inside Iranian airspace. As of 1983, this was not feasible, because Il-76s would be easy prey for Iranian interceptors. Therefore, the IrAF requested that the French find a different solution: the result was the adaptation of the same Douglas/Intertechnique D-704 pod to the Mirage F.1EQ-4, which could thus serve as a tanker for other F.1EQ-4s. This is how the IrAF organised and flew all of its long-range air strikes against Iran in 1986–1988.[3]

While the adaptation of Mirages for the tanker role proved a success, operating single-engined fighter-bombers over ranges of 700 and more kilometres, at altitudes of less than 50 metres, and in multiple in-flight refuelling operations, proved not only a demanding task for the involved pilots, but outright hazardous. Correspondingly, throughout the rest of the war with Iran, the IrAF continued searching for a better solution. In 1986, it acquired four Xian H-6D bombers from China. Based on the Soviet Tupolev Tu-16 medium bomber, these aircraft represented a specialised anti-ship variant: they were equipped with the Type 246 surveillance radar, capable of detecting large surface targets from as far as 150 kilometres away and were armed with CHETA YJ-6L anti-ship missiles (exported under the designation C.601) with a range of 120 kilometres. The unit operating them, No. 10 Squadron, was declared operational on the new type in December 1987, and flew about two dozen long-range anti-ship strikes into the lower Persian Gulf in 1988. This gave birth to the idea to convert an obsolete Tupolev Tu-16 bomber into a tanker through the installation of the necessary piping and one D-704 pod under each of its wingtips. Initiated in 1988, this project was concluded in 1989, and flight tested – with success – several times. However, the IrAF never got an opportunity to put it to use in actual combat, and the entire fleet of H-6Ds and Tu-16s was destroyed in air strikes during the 1991 war.

4
LATIN AMERICAN CONNECTION

In July 1976, the Brazilian corporation Petrobras discovered the huge Majnoon oilfield, near the border with Iran, and concluded a deal to extract 700,000 barrels of crude a day, most of which was to be exported to Brazil. From that point onwards, representatives of the government in Brasilia did their utmost to convince the Iraqis to buy products from the Brazilian defence sector as a compensation. The MIC was not easy to convince, and thus initial results were meagre: by 1980, Baghdad only placed an order for 2,000 military trucks, and 200 Engesa EE-9 Cascavel armoured cars and 200 EE-11 Urutu armoured personnel carriers of Brazilian origin. However, the situation was to experience a dramatic change through the onset of the Iran–Iraq War: not only did the government in Baghdad become keen to find yet additional alternative sources of arms, but it began receiving indirect support from an entirely unexpected direction: the United States of America. The crucial personalities in the establishment of the resulting Latin American connection included not only US President Ronald Reagan, and the contemporary director of the Central Intelligence Agency (CIA) of the USA, but also the Iraqi *Charge d'Affaires* at the embassy in Washington, Nizar Hamdoon – widely described as 'one of the most skilled lobbyist in town' of the early 1980s.

During his public appearances in Washington DC, Hamdoon loved to demonstratively pull out a green scarf reportedly recovered from the body of an IRGC soldier killed during the war, and decorated with a map of the Middle East, with numerous arrows all pointing at *al-Qods* – Jerusalem. Hamdoon's presentations at dinner parties and during congressional hearings eventually had the desired effect: in 1981, the Reagan Administration introduced the clandestine policy of assisting Iraq as a counterbalance to Iranian power. Amongst others, CIA director William Casey was advised to find a way to supply military intelligence, advice, and weaponry to Baghdad. While the US authorities were advised to 'turn a blind eye' to any possible Iraq-related activities of local companies, direct arms deliveries remained the subject of prohibition. Therefore, CIA director William Casey began either nudging the Iraqis in the direction of Latin American arms producers or helping them establish the necessary links.

CARDOEN'S BOMBS

In 1982 the Iraqis established links to the US-educated Chilean tycoon Carlos Cardoen. Ruled by fascist dictator General Augusto Pinochet since 1973, Chile was subjected to an international arms embargo and forced to develop its own defence sector – even more so when the country found itself at odds with Argentina in the late 1970s. By 1981, Industrias Cardoen SA was – amongst others – manufacturing general purpose, high-explosive, fragmentation bombs based on the design of the US-made Mk.80 bomb series (including Mk.82, Mk.83, and Mk.84), and several types of so-called cluster bomb units (CBUs; essentially, air-dropped weapons releasing submunitions). The design of any CBU was always a complex matter, for the weapon had to have a lightweight casing capable of withstanding high acceleration and air friction while hung on a high-speed combat aircraft, while also remaining capable of dispersing its cargo of submunitions over a wide area. Furthermore, the mass of bomblets in use during the 1970s had a specialised purpose: they were either developed for anti-tank, anti-personnel, or incendiary tasks, but none for all of these tasks at once.

Working on the basis of the US-made Mk.12 Rockeye CBU, engineers at Industrias Cardoen SA first developed the lightweight CB-100 and CB-130, suitable for deployment from older, US-made fighter-bomber types in service with the Chilean air force. Both weapons were filled with indigenously designed, self-propelled, multi-purpose PM-1 bomblets. Only 0.384m long, and having a body diameter of about 48mm, these weighed barely 0.8kg but were capable – upon the weapon's release – of fanning out to increase their effective coverage. Foremost, the design of the PM-1s included a probe to produce a hollow-charge effect enabling them to penetrate 150mm of mild steel armour, and the pre-fragmented body provided an anti-personnel capability. Finally, an incendiary element included 0.008kg of Zirconium – a rare material intensifying burning. Their fuse activated 1.5 seconds after release.

Once the first two CBU designs were in operational service, the Chileans embarked on a project for the development of more advanced and heavier variants. Thus came into being the CB-250-K and the CB-500: while sharing the overall design based on the Mk.12 (including a cruciform tail assembly with tip-out fins), their casings were made of high-resistance glass fibre, and had a tapered nose fitted with a fuse. Both weapons were outfitted with standard NATO 356mm, Soviet 250mm, and British-made single-suspension lugs, which made them compatible with a wide range of fighter-bombers in service in the 1970s and 1980s. The 250kg CB-500K was filled with 240 PM-1s. It incorporated an electronically programmed fuse which offered variable opening delay times and distributed bomblets along an elliptical pattern over an area of 50,000 square metres (including a central zone of

Two of the CBUs designed by Cardoenas seen installed on the centreline pylon of a Mirage 50 of the Chilean Air Force. (via Ali Tobchi)

'severe destruction' of about 20,000 square metres). The CB-250-K was an advanced model: about 2.46m long, it weighed only 227kg while still filled with 240 PM-1s. It had about the same destructive pattern as the CB-500, but a much higher range of delivery methods, including a minimum release altitude of 75m at speeds between 300 and 530 knots. Unsurprisingly, the CB-250-K was considered to be one of the most advanced CBUs of its time, outmatching the performance of much heavier US, British, French, or comparable Soviet designs – and this at only about 35 percent of the unit price (for example, a single CB-250-K cost about FF40,000, in comparison to FF150,000 for a single Matra BLG-66 Belouga manufactured in France).

Once Hamdoon linked-up Cardoen with the MIC, a contract was signed for the delivery of CB-250s via a Miami-based Swissco Management Group (controlled by Cardoen). The first shipment of Chilean-made CBUs reached Iraq in 1984, on board an Ilyushin Il-76 transport aircraft of the Iraqi Air Force (even if wearing the livery of Iraqi Airlines). The weapon entered operational service with

Carlos Cardoen (left) with Saddam Hussein. (US Department of Commerce)

A row of Cardoen's CB-250s, as put on display during the May 1989 arms fair in Baghdad. (via Ali Tobchi)

Mirage-equipped units of the IrAF before the end of the same year, and several additional orders were to follow over the next two years.

Although the IrAF constantly complained about the poor manufacturing quality of the CB-250 – casings that failed to open and disperse their bomblets on release; bomblets that failed to detonate; bombs that went out of control and damaged the aircraft releasing them (and the Iraqis are known to have lost at least two fighter-bombers in such accidents) – by 1985 the MIC decided to launch licence production of CB-250s and CB-500s in Iraq. Appearing easy 'on paper', this was a complex enterprise, which required not only the import of the machinery and tools necessary for the construction and equipment of the an-Numan Works within ar-Rashid Camp (reportedly worth about US$60 million), and at the Qaqaa Complex, but also the import of materials like munitions-grade zirconium, which intensified burning and thus helped to penetrate armour. Thus, and amongst others, Swissco, Cardoen, and the MIC arranged a deal in which 100 tons of zirconium (worth about US$2 million) were exported to Iraq by the US company Teledyne Wah Chang Inc. – via Chile, with official approval and export licences of the Commerce Department.

The an-Numan Works initiated production of CB-250Ks in 1987; by the following year, the MIC is known to have paid about US$200 million to Chile for Cardoen's bombs; and by 1990 two other factories in Iraq became involved in the project. Iraq thus became only the second country in the Middle East – right after Israel – manufacturing its own CBUs.[1]

PROJECT 395

In the 1970s, the military junta in power in Argentina launched the development of nuclear weapons. Such a project required a 'delivery platform', and thus the Argentine Air Force (FAA) was tasked with developing a suitable ballistic missile. Lacking the know-how and technology, the Argentineans decided to import these from West Germany. With their country being subjected to a growing number of import restrictions, in 1979, the FAA signed a contract with Consen, a consortium of 16 companies based in Zug, Switzerland, which was to act as a front to disguise the acquisition, transfer, and import of sensitive technologies, materials, machinery, and tools. Henceforth, Consen acted as a 'project leader'. This company established business links with several 'giants' in the defence sector of Western Europe, including Messerschmitt-Bölkow-Blohm (MBB) and MAN in West Germany, Sagem in France, subsidiaries of Fiat in Italy, and many others, and about a dozen enterprises in the USA. The result of this effort was the missile named Condor I, which proved to have relatively little military capability, but could still deliver a payload of up to 400kg over a range of 150km. By 1983, the project was thus expanded into the version named Condor IAIII, or *Alcaràn*.

By this time, the MIC was informed about the work in Argentina and – with Amer Rashid all the time stressing the importance of Iraq launching domestic production of ballistic missiles – the first links were established between Baghdad and Buenos Aires. When the Argentineans introduced the director of the MIC and his 'right hand', Lieutenant General Amer as-Saadi (a chemist educated in Germany, with experience from working at the Yarmouk Factory, and specialised in solid-fuels for rockets), the two proved disappointed with the Condor I. The head of the Argentine team, Colonel Guerrero, then suggested that they convert the existing missile into a second stage, add a liquid-fuelled first stage, and that such a weapon should be capable of reaching a range between 800 and 1,500km. This was something of special interest for Amer Rashid and Saadi, and thus an agreement was reached for Iraq to finance the continuation of the Argentine project in the form of a much more powerful missile, the Condor II – which, essentially, was based on the design of the US-made MGM-31 Pershing II.[2] Because the Iraqis knew that their involvement would promptly attract far too much attention, they decided to make use of Egypt and the AOI as a front, with Baghdad remaining in the background and 'only' providing the funding. After a series of urgent conferences between Egyptian and Iraqi representatives, the resulting contract – between the Egyptian Ministry of Defence and Consen's subsidiary Institute of Advanced Technology (IFAT) – was signed on 15 February 1984. In Iraq, this enterprise received the codename Project 395.

PROJECT SAAD-16

Right from the start, Project Condor II/395 included the acquisition of a double, if not triple set of all the related machinery and tools: after all, Amer Rashid and Saadi wanted to set up a production facility for the missile in Iraq, and, certainly enough, the Egyptians were as keen to exploit the opportunity. That said, the MIC was ready to go much further than just enter a secret alliance with the Argentineans: in 1983, Amer Rashid initiated Project Saad-16, which stipulated the construction of a facility for missile research, development and testing outside Mosul. A suitable partner was found in Bielefeld, in Germany, in the form of the company Gildmeister Projecta (GIPRO). On 16 January 1984, the MIC and GIPRO signed a contract worth about US$253 million, for the design and construction of the facility. Eventually, 38 German companies and several Austrian companies became involved in Project Saad-16, resulting in probably the biggest and most sophisticated factory of its kind in the Middle East, including numerous underground workshops, installations and bunkers, all connected by underground tunnels, its own hospital and a fire brigade, and a 100-metre-long missile assembly hall. By the time it was completed, up to 40 percent of the equipment was provided by US companies. For example, Hewlett-Packard provided computers for some 50 laboratories in the complex, while others provided a scalar analyser system, computer graphics terminals, measuring instruments, and telecommunications and satellite ground-station equipment.

As soon as the contract was signed, the Argentineans launched work on the new missile at their research facility in Falda del Carmen, in the Sierra Chica mountains, with related tests carried out at El Chamical Air Force Testing Ground. Whether the original aim was really to first develop a single stage missile, then two and three stages remains unclear: what is certain is that thanks to the involvement of Cairo, the MIC – acting through the AOI and Arab League Industrial Development Organisation – experienced no problems while setting up the cover for its activities: its representatives established Consen, a Swiss-based consortium, including 16 companies distributed all over Western Europe. These first began contracting some of the top European arms producers, including MBB and MAN of Germany, Sagem of France, and subsidiaries of Italy's Fiat, before entering cooperation with numerous smaller enterprises on that continent, and about a dozen companies from the USA.

Eventually, the Argentineans developed the Condor II: an 11-metre-long, 6,500kg, two-stage missile roughly resembling the US-made Pershing II, and expected to become capable of delivering a 500kg cluster munition warhead over a range between 800 and 1,000km. By 1985, this had progressed sufficiently for the MIC to officially sign a related contract and assign it the codename Project 395, and to initiate the next step: the construction of a plant for the production of a solid-propellant rocket motor for a missile that in Egypt and Iraq was to carry the designation Badr-2000. Largely unnoticed, or at least 'ignored' by the authorities in most of the countries involved, high-technology production equipment and tools for the fabrication of the first solid-propellant stage – worth about US$400 million – were all imported and in place by early 1989, by when a factory for the production of suitable chemicals was completed within the al-Qaʿqaa complex, while a new research and development facility and test stand were constructed in northern Iraq.

Much to the disappointment of Baghdad, it was precisely around this time that Project 395 encountered several problems. Correspondingly, in 1987, Iraq signed another contract for the provision of only 17 complete Badr-2000 missiles and ground support equipment.

In January 1988, Egypt and Iraq launched a joint clandestine effort to acquire high-technology equipment and materials for missile development. The project was conducted by the Egyptian Minister of Defence General Abdel Halim Abu Ghazzala, who appointed Colonel Hussam Youssef as his emissary in Europe. Youssef opened an office in Salzburg, in Austria, from where he directed a ring of agents all over the West, including the USA. Amongst those involved in the operation was Abdel Kader Helmy, an Egyptian-born rocket scientist who lived in California and was recruited to source rocket fuel chemicals, carbon-fibre materials, steel for rocket casings, telemetry tracking equipment and assembly plans for a tactical missile system. Finding it easy to buy almost everything, Helmy placed orders worth nearly US$1 million in a matter of a few months. Everything was shipped to Baltimore International Airport, where it was to be picked up by a Lockheed C-130 Hercules transport of the Egyptian Air Force, bound for Cairo. It was at this point that the notorious Israeli foreign secret service Mossad became involved: it not only placed a remote tracker in the

car of one of the Egyptian agents in Germany, but also tipped off US Customs that Helmy was running an illegal operation obtaining restricted missile technology and smuggling it to Egypt. Before long, his telephone was tapped by the FBI just as he collected a total of 28 tons of rocket fuel, 195 kilogram of carbon-carbon fibre matting (used as a protective coating for ballistic missile warheads), rocket motor nozzles, and 40 sheets of military-grade high nickel-content steel with special forgings enabling the Egyptians and Iraqis to bend and weld large rocket motor casings. Helmy was arrested on 24 June 1988, and Ghazzala's ring effectively smashed by the US authorities.

Later the same year, severe disputes between Argentina, Egypt and Iraq interrupted their cooperation: the Argentineans had failed to produce the guidance system they had promised, and the Egyptians had failed to acquire the high-technology materials they were supposed to supply. Unsurprisingly, a dummy test in Argentina – which included launch-preparation and software trials – exposed numerous and significant technical problems. According to the Iraqis, the MIC terminated the project in late 1988, Baghdad deciding to complete the Badr-2000 – and especially the production of a solid-propellant rocket motor – on its own. The Argentineans reported a sole test flight in 1989, but that the missile flew only about 500km, and the development was still incomplete when, in early 1990, Buenos Aires terminated all the remaining work under severe pressure from the USA.

By this time, the MIC was attempting to complete Project 395 entirely on its own. Initially, the Iraqis were successful in signing contracts with most of the original contractors and relaunched the programme using whatever documentation for the semi-finished

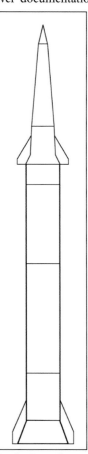

A simplified diagram of the Condor II missile. It was 10.4m long, had a diameter of 0.8m, and weighed about 5,200kg at launch. With a payload of 500kg it was expected to become capable of reaching at least 800–900km range. The system was intended to be road-mobile, but nothing is known about how far the Iraqis – or Egyptians – got with work on the related TEL. (Diagram by Tom Cooper)

weapon had already been transferred – which was not much: while having received most of the technical specifications, due to the failure of Ghazzala's clandestine operation Iraq could not obtain the carbon-carbon to make the nose cone. Moreover, soon after Iraqi representatives began to deal directly with suppliers in Western Europe and elsewhere, numerous intelligence agencies were alerted, and the acquisition of the necessary technology greatly slowed down, and then entirely stopped. Although additional equipment was imported clandestinely through 1990, Project 395 thus began lagging behind the plan and then came to a full stop. Ultimately, it was never completed. Indeed, even the integration facilities at the al-Qaqaa Complex remained incomplete, and although at least one solid-fuel motor was tested in 1989, not a single Badr-2000 missile was ever assembled in Iraq. While about 30 missile assembly sets were completed in Argentina by 1991, they all lacked their guidance components: the last two were destroyed in the late 1990s.

PROJECT 200

Parallel to the Badr, Iraq ran a project to import solid-fuel technology from Germany and Italy, via Egypt, for a short-range (120km) ballistic missile named the FK.120 or Sakr 200. Although potential sources in Europe were found, all of these refused to provide production capability, and the Egyptians were thus capable only of passing along some of the related design information to the Iraqis. Eventually, the project ended nowhere, and all the related facilities were bombed out in 1991.

5
MULTIPLE ROCKET LAUNCHERS

As described in a previous chapter, Iraq had established good cooperation with Brazil in 1976, and began importing Brazilian-made arms and military equipment a few years later. The closeness of this relationship became even more important during the Soviet arms embargo – lasting from September 1980 until May 1981 – imposed after the Iraqi invasion of Iran and was then further intensified during the following year, resulting in several little-known or misinterpreted projects.

THE PROTOTYPE DEAL

Threats to 'export' the 'Islamic' revolution in a western direction, expressed time and again once Khomeini took over in Tehran, were not only taken seriously by Iraq, but also caused continuously growing concern amongst Iran's neighbours on the western side of the Persian Gulf. In early 1981, Saudi Arabia, Kuwait, Bahrain, Qatar, Oman, and the United Arab Emirates (UAE) created the Gulf Cooperation Council (GCC), with the aim of pooling resources and improving their mutual protection. Iraq was not a member, but members of the GCC began supporting Baghdad's war effort through

granting ever greater loans and using the AOI to exercise political and economic influence upon the Western powers. Over the following two years, this resulted in a number of large arms deals organised in an unusual fashion. In almost every case, Egypt – officially still excluded from the Arab League and under a diplomatic blockade for signing the Camp David Accords with Israel in 1979 – served as the front through which Kuwait, Saudi Arabia, and the UAE would finance arms orders for Iraq.

The first such deal was negotiated and signed by representatives from Baghdad, Cairo, and Paris between November 1981 and February 1982: Egypt was to receive Dassault Mirage 2000 interceptors and Iraq additional Mirage F.1EQ-4 fighter-bombers, which were to be paid for by Kuwait and Riyadh in crude oil. This arrangement became a prototype for numerous similar orders placed over the following years.

PIRANHA

While involved in negotiations for additional Mirage F.1EQ fighter-bombers, in late 1981 representatives of the MIC were informed that the Brazilians were working on several of their own, indigenous designs. One was the Engesa EE-T1 Osório main battle tank, purposely designed for export to 'Third World countries', as a cheaper alternative to Soviet and Western models. Unable to finance the research and development of this project on their own, the Brazilians were keen to attract the attention of the MIC and an agreement was reached for one of two prototypes to be sent to Iraq for testing. Rather quickly, the Iraqi Army concluded that the 41-ton, but lightly armoured Osório was no match for the Soviet-made T-72, which proved effective in early battles with Iranians. Thus, no agreement on acquisition was ever reached. Other Brazilian ideas proved much more interesting, though. One was to help Iraq launch domestic production of 57mm unguided rockets of Brazilian design, custom tailored for deployment from Soviet pods like the UB-16-57 and UB-32-57, which were in widespread use on combat aircraft of the Iraqi Air Force, especially the MiG-21, MiG-23, Su-7, Su-20 and Su-22. This project was realised and Iraq eventually launched production of 57mm rockets of Brazilian design at home.

An EE-9 Cascavel armoured car, designed and produced in Brazil. The vehicle proved highly efficient in Libyan service in desert conditions during the short war between Egypt and Libya in 1977, attracting Iraqi attention. Iraq thus placed an order for 200 Cascavels and 200 EE-11 Urutu armoured personnel carriers in the same year. (via Ali Tobchi)

An MAA-1 Piranha AAM installed on the wingtip station of a Northrop F-5E Tiger II fighter-bomber of the Brazilian Air Force. (Photo by Henrique L Martins, via Alfredo André)

A front view of the seeker-head of the MAA-1 Piranha – the part of the weapon that caused most trouble to the Brazilians: the MIC was particularly keen to obtain the know-how and technology for the development and production of such high-tech systems. (Photo by Henrique L Martins via Alfredo André)

For comparison, this photograph shows the MAA-1B Piranha, developed in the 2000s in cooperation between Brazil and South Africa. (Photo by Henrique L Martins, via Alfredo André)

The third Brazilian project to attract Iraqi attention in the early 1980s was one for an infrared homing, air-to-air missile, designated MAA-1 Piranha. The weapon – roughly comparable in shape and size to the US-made AIM-9 Sidewinder but expected to be faster – had been undergoing development since 1976, but progressed very slowly due to the lack of funding and the necessary know-how, a severe economic crisis in Brazil and a US arms embargo. Of critical importance was the technology for the seeker head, which no foreign companies were ready to supply – at least not at prices acceptable to the Brazilians. However, when a Brazilian trade delegation visited Baghdad in November 1981, it quickly found out that the MIC was keen to fund further research and development of the MAA-1.[1]

The Iraqi – i.e. Saudi and Kuwaiti – funding not only saved the Brazilian project: it enabled the establishment of Órbita – a state-owned company responsible for further development of the Piranha – and the acquisition of the necessary high-tech, either from France or somewhere else. As a result of this enterprise, the company D. F. Vasconcellos (which manufactured night-vision binoculars, and telescopic sights for the Cascavel armoured cars already in service with the Iraqi Army) was contracted with the development of the seeker head. By 1984, the Piranha was thus 'back on track', and the first test-firing took place two years later. By 1988, the project had reached an advanced stage and a team of Brazilian rocket scientists was deployed to Iraq to help set up local production facilities.[2]

It was the Iraqi invasion of Kuwait of August 1990, and the following total arms embargo imposed by the UN, that delivered the proverbial 'nail in the coffin' of the idea to complete the development of the Piranha and set up its production in Iraq. Baghdad had to stop financing the project, the Brazilians were sent back home, and further development of the missile slowed down to a crawling pace – resulting in the MAA-1 becoming outdated and de-facto cancelled. In the 1990s, the Brazilian Air Force opted to buy Israeli-made Python-3 missiles instead. It was more than 10 years later that the project was relaunched under the designation MAA-1B, and then with some help from South Africa. Exactly how many Piranhas were ever manufactured, and if they really entered service with the Brazilian Air Force remains unclear.[3]

ASTROS

In addition to becoming involved in funding the Piranha, in November 1981 the MIC placed an order for 66 Avibrás SS-30 Astros II multiple rocket launcher systems. Mounted on a 6x6 truck designed by Mercedes-Benz, the SS-30 launcher had 32 tubes of 127mm calibre, the rockets of which could reach a range of 27km. Over the following years, the MIC funded its further development, resulting in variants designated SS-40 (with sixteen 180mm rockets and range of 40km) and SS-60 (with four 300mm rockets and range of 70km). For unknown reasons, development of the SS-30 took years, and it was only in 1986 that the first SS-30 reached Iraq. They

were rushed to the southern battlefield during the same year, with unknown results.

What is certain is that although the Iraqis sent five of their engineers to Brazil for training in the production of the related rockets, in 1989 the MIC eventually abandoned the idea of production of SS-30s, SS-40s, and SS-60s at home. Nevertheless, the deployment of the Astros with the Iraqi Army encouraged a number of the armed forces of the Gulf Cooperation Council (GCC) to follow up, and thus Saudi Arabia, Bahrain, and Qatar placed orders for the SS-30, SS-40, and SS-60, making the system one of Avibrás's biggest commercial successes of the 1980s.

PROJECT ORKAN

The reason why the Iraqis decided not to launch licence production of the Brazilian-made MRLS was that in the meantime they had found a source of cheaper, far simpler to operate, yet more capable weapons of that kind – in Yugoslavia. In 1986, the Military Technical Institute in Belgrade and the MIC initiated Project KOL-15, aiming to develop a multiple rocket launcher capable of precisely striking targets 50 kilometres away. Two prototypes were developed early on – one for Iraq and one for Yugoslavia – each installed on the chassis of an 8x8 FAP 3232 heavy off-road truck (one of the most sophisticated trucks in its class of the time, based on a design by Mercedes-Benz). Designated the LRSV-262, each firing unit weighed about 15,000kg, included twelve 262mm calibre launch tubes, and was equipped with a reloading crane. On Iraqi insistence, all the firing units and trucks carrying reloads were designed on the same chassis, and very compact, so to be easily disguised as 'regular cargo trucks', and capable of very quick reloading. By 1987, the system was ready for series production and introduced to operations by the Yugoslav National Army as the M-87 Orkan. At the time, it was one of the most advanced MRLSs in world-wide service and thanks to very precise automatic levelling and automatic barrel sighting, it could be brought into action within less than five minutes from stopping. Launch tubes made of hard-chromed barrels required no cleaning after firing, and with the help of

An Iraqi-operated SS-30 Astros II Mk 3 multiple rocket launch system in action in 1987. (US DoD)

A close-up view of an Astros II Mk 3 launcher. For quicker reloading, weapons were prepacked in containers that included their launch tubes and rockets. As a result, the same launcher could deploy all calibres of rocket eventually developed for the system, including SS-30, SS-40, SS-60, and SS-80. (US DoD)

The second LRSV-262 prototype, which was deployed for extensive testing in high temperatures in Iraq during 1987. Notable is the compact design on the chassis of the 8x8 heavy off-road truck, which meant that while on the move the vehicle could be easily disguised as 'another cargo truck'. (Yugoslav MOD, via Ali Tobchi)

anti-tank mines equipped with a non-magnetic action fuse.

Following over 500 test-firings in Yugoslavia (including several rounds with 'special' warheads), in August 1987 one of the LRSV-262 prototypes and 500 R-262 rockets were brought to Iraq for testing under desert conditions – apparently completed by a short combat deployment in the Basra area. Both the Iraqi Army and the MIC proved so enthusiastic as to promptly place and order for an unknown quantity of Orkans under the Iraqi designation Ababil-50. Furthermore, on Iraqi request, the Yugoslavs developed six variants of its 4.6-metre-long 390kg rockets (designated R-262), equipped with at least six types of warheads, including high-explosive fragmentation, cluster, and mine warheads; and launched the development of a variant capable of reaching the range of 65km.[4]

the crane installed on the LSRV-262, the reloading process took less than two minutes. Finally, the version of the R-262 rocket equipped with a cluster warhead was capable of dispersing up to 24 KPOM

The standard range of the R-262 rockets was 50km and the system proved much simpler to maintain and operate than the SS-30 Astros. Instead of using modular launchers, instrumental navigation system supported by GPS, and rockets made of composites, it employed a very precise alignment of the launcher (possible thanks to the design, construction and equipment of every single LRSV-262) to obtain impressive precision. That said, production at the factory in Novi Travnik (nowadays in Bosnia Herzegovina) progressed very slowly. The first battery destined for Iraq – including four self-propelled launchers, four resupply vehicles (each with 24 rockets)

Test-firing of an R-262 rocket from the second prototype of the LRSV-262 in the desert of western Iraq. (Yugoslav MOD)

A still from a video showing an LRSV-262 firing unit of the M-87 system during the war in the former Yugoslavia in the 1990s. Notably, in this image the launcher is elevated almost to the maximum. (Yugoslav MOD)

Two stills from a video showing one of four operational Ababil-50s in Iraq. The driver's cabin was fully air-conditioned. The armament of the single LRSV-262 firing unit was completed by a single 7.62mm anti-aircraft machine gun (not visible in these stills). (Iraqi National TV)

and a consignment of about 1,000 R-262 rockets – was delivered only in early 1990. While these promptly entered operational service, this was the end of the growth of Iraq's Ababil-50 force. Probably due to the growing disorder and political unrest in Yugoslavia, the production rate in Novi Travnik decreased significantly. By early 1992, only eight additional LRSV-262s and two command vehicles were completed: the outbreak of the war in Bosnia then resulted in these being distributed between Croat and Bosnian Muslim forces. Meanwhile, a consignment of 800 R-262 rockets destined for Iraq and stored in the port of Ploce while waiting for its shipment to Iraq (stopped because of the UN arms embargo imposed following Iraqi invasion of Kuwait, in August 1990), was partially withdrawn to Serbia and partially destroyed by the Yugoslav Air Force early during the war in Croatia in the summer of 1991.

6
BULL'S GUNS

Quite early during the war with Iran, the Iraqi Army reached the unpleasant conclusion that the Iranian artillery – the mass of which was of US origin and self-propelled – was not only longer-ranged, but also more mobile and firing shells filled with explosives more effective than its own, the mass of which was of Soviet origin. Moreover, Moscow was reluctant to deliver 50 each of the 122mm 2S1 Gvozdika and 152mm 2S3 Akatsiya self-propelled howitzers ordered in 1978: as of summer 1980, only two batteries of these were in service (with the 6th Armoured Division), and none saw action before 1982. Unsurprisingly, the MIC was on a search for superior artillery pieces within weeks of the onset of the war: before long, they came across the designs of Canadian engineer Gerald Vincent Bull.

PREQUEL

Born in 1928, Bull graduated in aeronautical engineering. A charismatic person of immense energy, he specialised in the design and construction of wind tunnels early on, before becoming involved in research and development of the Velvet Glove, a short-range semi-active radar homing air-to-air missile designed by the Canadian Armament Research and Development Establishment (CARDE, nowadays DRDC Valcrtier) in the early 1950s. Despite significant investment, the Velvet Glove was cancelled while still undergoing aerodynamic testing in 1954, in favour of the outperforming, active radar homing XAAM-N-2a/AAM-N-3 Sparrow II from the USA. Ironically, the US missile experienced massive delays and was then cancelled only two years later, but Bull was meanwhile busy further developing his aerodynamic tunnel, working on anti-ballistic missiles, and, in 1956 he launched work on a high-velocity gun capable of launching a satellite. In the early 1960s, he secured US funding under the High Altitude Research Project (HARP) from the Pentagon, and received the first of eventually three US-made 16-inch (406mm) battleship guns to conduct related testing. Because the 406mm guns were too large for his privately owned test-site near Highwater in Quebec, he arranged a new test-site in Barbados. This became operational in early 1962 and was used for test-firing 127mm dart-like finned projectiles named Martlet. Still financed by the Pentagon, by 1963 Bull developed the Martlet-3 full bore projectile, which proved capable of reaching altitudes of 249km (155 miles). However, the Canadian never managed to reach his actual aim, the development of a three-stage, gun-fired 16.4in rocket – the Martlet-4 – that would enable Canada to enter the space-launch business. The project was cancelled due to fierce opposition from

major arms manufacturers in the USA; budget overruns; changing public attitudes towards military affairs; negative reviews from the press and other researchers in Canada; and changes in government policies. Back to Canada in 1968–69, he set up a new company – the Space Research Corporation (SRC) – with the aim of focusing on research and development of high-velocity artillery and providing consultancy on artillery-related issues on the international level.[1]

GC-45

It was under these circumstances that in the early 1970s the Pentagon approached Bull with a request to develop a gun capable of countering Soviet-made 130mm M-54 guns, which – with their range of 30,000m (18.64 miles) – easily outmatched the 127mm guns of the US Navy's warships. The Canadian's solution was the development of a new 155mm gun, as in widespread use by dozens of Western armed forces. After concluding that sub-calibre sabot rounds offered a much better range performance, but carried too little explosive power, Bull refocused on designing a new aerodynamically superior, extended range full bore 155mm shell. This resulted in the emergence of a design made of extremely hard 9260 steel, which proved capable of travelling one and a half times farther while shattering into three times more fragments than standard NATO shells in service at the time. Encouraged by the results, in 1973 the Belgian company Poudreriers Réunies de Belgíque (PRB) contracted SRC to develop two new types of 155mm guns: one designed to be towed, and the other with its own built-in transportation. The result was the design named Gun Calibre 45 (GC-45), with 45 referring to the length of the barrel: the gun calibre was 155mm and the barrel length was 45 calibres – or 6,975mm (almost seven metres).[2]

THE NORICUM AFFAIR

The GC-45 and its shells proved a major commercial success: during the 1970s, the SRC flourished from selling their designs to several customers abroad, including Austria, Israel, the People's Republic of China, and South Africa. While the Israelis were keen to obtain the design for the extended range full bore ammunition – which their company Soltam adapted for use with US-made 175mm M107 and 155mm M109 self-propelled howitzers – the Austrians and South Africans went a step further. Noricum – the arms division of the state-owned steel company Voest-Alpine – purchased the design of the GC-45 installed on a mount with four wheels: nominally, this was truck-towed, but the carriage included a small diesel engine that drove the hydraulics of the gun and was adapted to act as an auxiliary propulsion unit capable of quickly redeploying it to a new firing position. Manufactured in series under the designation GHN-45, this weapon had a range of up to 29,900 metres with extended range full bore ammunition (ERFB), no less than 39,600 metres with base-bleed ammunition, or 50,000 metres (31 miles) using rocket-assisted V-LAP rounds – which quickly earned it numerous export orders. Following extensive testing, the Denel SOC Ltd Company of South Africa procured barrels, 30,000 rounds and design specifications for the GC-45. These served as prototypes that eventually led to the famous G-5 gun – which entered operational service with the South African Defence Forces in 1982, and, in 1986–1988, the G-6 Rhino self-propelled howitzer.

Unsurprisingly, Bull's designs attracted Iraqi attention and during the same year SRC was contacted by Amer Rashid. Negotiations resulted in an order worth US$300 million for 300 GHN-45s manufactured in Austria and 41,000 155mm shells manufactured by PRB in Belgium. The first shipment of GHN-45s reached Iraq

An Iraqi GHN-45, at the Royal Armouries in Great Britain, following its capture during the war for the liberation of Kuwait in 1991. This photograph shows the weapon in transport configuration: in firing configuration, the barrel would be turned 180 degrees away from the two trail arms. (Photo by Ted Hooton)

in 1984, under the guise of a delivery to Jordan. A few years later, this caused a major scandal in Austria where arms export laws prohibited any deliveries to countries in a state of war.

PROJECT SHERI

The GHN-45 quickly proved capable of outranging Iranian M107s, M109s and M110s, and – initially – the Iraqis were delighted with its performance. However, very soon they

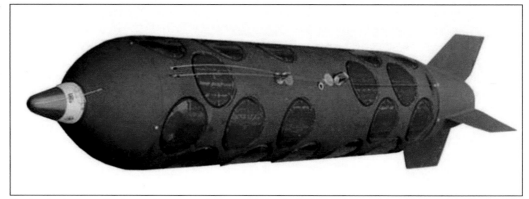

The South African-made CB.470 CBU, exported to Iraq and also manufactured there under licence. The weapon was primarily deployed by Mirage F.1EQs, but also by Soviet-made Sukhoi Su-22 and Su-25 fighter-bombers. (Denel)

realised that shells of Bull's design were very hard on barrels: the frequent use of long-range shells required the more frequent replacement of the barrels and they tended to wear out after firing between 600 and 700 rounds, which was much less than the 1,500 stipulated in the contract between the MIC and Noricum. With Iraq lacking the capability to launch production of such barrels at home, in 1984 Amer Rashid cancelled the contract with Noricum and instead placed an order for 250 G-5 guns from South Africa, together with equipment and machinery necessary for their production and that of their ammunition and shells in Iraq. As far as is known, deliveries of these were interrupted by the UN arms embargo imposed in reaction to the Iraqi invasion of Kuwait on 2 August 1990, by when about 110 G-5s were in service with artillery units of the Iraqi Republican Guards. In Iraqi service, the G-5s became known as Sheri. That said, Amer Rashid's decision to cancel the contract for the GHN-45 also had negative repercussions for Iraq: having a stock of 110 already manufactured guns, the Austrians found a way to sell these to Iran – via Libya – instead.

JUPITER FUSES AND SCB.470

Around the time Amer Rashid was negotiating the acquisition of G-5s – in 1984 – a delegation from the Iraqi Air Force visited Morocco and, amongst others, saw Mirage F.1CH/EH fighter-bombers of the local air force armed with South African-made bombs based on the design of the US-made Mk.80 series, including bombs such as the Mk.82 (250kg/500lbs), Mk.83 (500kg/1,000lbs), and Mk.84 (1,000kg/2,000lbs). Moreover, they noticed that the

Moroccans were making extensive use of Jupiter fuses, which could be set to detonate their bombs several metres above the ground (or the sea), thus greatly expanding their destructive radius. The result of this experience was two-fold: the Iraqis not only began ordering bombs based on the design of the Mk.80 series from Portugal and Spain, but also placed a huge order for Jupiter fuses in South Africa. In turn, Amer Rashid was informed about the CB.470 cluster bomb units designed and manufactured in South Africa, and promptly placed not only an order for these, but acquired the licence for their production in Iraq under the local designation SCB.470. This was launched in 1987, in the an-Numan factory, constructed at Camp Rashid, in Baghdad.[3]

Cooperation between the MIC and South African defence sector continued over the following years and at least until 1990, by when the two launched the joint development of an unmanned aerial vehicle (UAV), equipped with a video-camera for reconnaissance purposes, and a datalink capable of transmitting the resulting videos to base in real time. A sub-variant of this project – the aerodynamic design was based on the delta-wing – was intended to have a warhead: the idea was that the weapon could, if it found a suitable target of opportunity worth expending it upon, be used for attack purposes. Ultimately, this highly promising project was abandoned due to the UN arms embargo of August 1990. However, and quite interestingly, a few years later Israel pressed into service its indigenous Harpy UAV, based on exactly the same concept – and the same aerodynamic design.

7

THE FIRST WAR OF THE CITIES

The urgency with which Iraq needed its weapon of deterrent – a ballistic missile capable of reaching Tehran – became obvious less than two years after Project Condor II was initiated. In late 1984, the General Military Intelligence Directorate of Iraq (GMID) obtained information that Mohsen Rafighdoost, the chief of Ayatollah Ruhollah Khomeini's security detail and Minister of the Islamic Revolutionary Guards Corps (IRGC), was authorised by the government in Tehran to travel abroad and obtain R-17E missiles, and to have the IRGC personnel trained to operate them. Rafighdoost visited Libya and Syria – both of which were at odds with Iraq and supporting Iran – and arranged for the delivery of two 9P117 TELs and 20 R-17Es. While IRGC personnel were trained abroad, Syrian specialists came to Iran to help establish a base for the newly established Khatam al-Anbya Missile Force of the IRGC in Khorramabad. The unit became operational in early 1985, and on 12 March 1985, it fired an R-17E missile against the oil refinery at Kirkuk. By this time, the government in Baghdad had convinced several allied Arab governments to exercise severe pressure upon Damascus to cease its support for Iran. Thus, the Syrian experts were withdrawn only days later. However, the IRGC's Scuds were now operational, and by June 1985 the Iranians fired 12 additional R-17Es at Iraqi population centres, causing hundreds of casualties, and significant material damage.

TEHRAN BLITZ

The appearance of Iranian Scuds exercised massive pressure upon the RCC and Saddam Hussein demanded that the Iraqi armed forces hit back in similar fashion. However, Tehran and other major cities in Iran were all outside their reach. This was the point in time at which the Iraqi ingenuity – possibly thanks to the massive investment and 15 years of training weapons specialists – became an important factor in this war for the first time. Within less than 24 hours of the first Iranian Scud strike on Kirkuk, the Technical Department of Taqaddum Air Base – the home base of Iraq's MiG-25 fleet – installed bomb shackles from Mirage F.1EQs and French-designed SAMP Type-21 400kg bombs under the wing of one of their MiG-25RBs.

Theoretically, this offered Iraq the capability to reach and to bomb Tehran – even if the Iraqis knew that such a mission would be extremely risky: Type-21 bombs lacked the thermal insulation necessary to protect the weapon from the high temperatures caused by air friction when the Foxbat was underway at Mach 2 and higher speeds. However, the commanders of the IrAF and the GMID were clever enough to outsmart the Soviets. Next morning, they took the Soviet Air Force Attaché to Baghdad for a visit to Taqaddum AB, the home base of Iraq's MiG-25 fleet. 'By sheer accident', the officer thus received a unique opportunity to see a MiG-25RB loaded with 'US-made bombs'. This operation had the desired effect: no sooner had the Soviet officer returned to the embassy in Baghdad, he made a call to report his sighting to Moscow. The next morning a Soviet Air Force transport aircraft arrived at Baghdad International Airport,

One of two 9P117 TELs acquired by the IRGC in early 1985, seen on the streets of Tehran. (Tom Cooper collection)

to deliver a load of FAB-500T insulated bombs and MBD3-U2T-1 multiple ejector racks with bomb shackles, necessary for their installation on the MiG-25RB.

In a matter of hours, the new equipment was rushed to Taqaddum AB and installed on one of the MiG-25RBs. By this time, the original Iraqi unit operating this type – No. 87 Squadron – had converted to MiG-25PD (export) interceptors, while an entirely new unit – No. 97 Squadron – was worked up to operate the reconnaissance-strike variant. But, after three years of maintaining the type, its technicians were highly experienced and there was no doubt that they were specially motivated, too. Thus, the same afternoon, 14 March 1985, Major Ummar boarded his MiG-25RB loaded with four FAB-500Ts, took off and flew away in to the east. Because the capital of Iran was at the very verge of the jet's range, his mission was particularly complex: Umar first transferred to the newly constructed Bakr AB, north-east of Baghdad (better known in the West as 'Balad'), to top off his fuel tanks, before flying the actual raid. After his second take-off, he penetrated Iranian airspace at low altitude, flying through a 'hole' in the IRIAF's radar coverage, and in between the peaks of the Zagros Mountains. Only once more than 100 kilometres deep inside Iran, did he initiate a gradual climb to the operational altitude of 21,000 metres, while accelerating to Mach 2.3. The target programmed into the Peleng-D navigational-attack system of his MiG-25RB was the High Command of the IRIAF at Dowshan Tappeh Air Base, in downtown Tehran. Because the Peleng was relatively primitive and actually meant for the deployment of tactical nuclear weapons, it was not particularly precise. Moreover, because Ummar released the bombload while underway at 21,000 metres and Mach 2.35 – and thus as far as 43–45 kilometres from the target – his attack proved imprecise: the four bombs fell into a residential area adjacent to the target. Nevertheless, the message was delivered, and in quite a spectacular fashion: Iraq now had the means to retaliate against Iranian strikes on Baghdad, and the IRIAF had no weapons on hand to counter these.

Two additional raids on Tehran were flown by MiG-25RBs of No. 97 Squadron on 16 March 1983 – both against Tehran. Subsequently, the unit split its effort in two: the Iranian capital remained the primary target of one flight, staffed by less-experienced pilots, while senior pilots flew air raids on Tabriz, Qom, Qazvin, Karaj, Rasht, and Hamedan. Every mission was undertaken by a single jet, always armed with four FAB-500Ts: larger warloads – usually: eight bombs (two under each wing, and four under the centreline) – were deployed only against targets closer to Iraq. As far as can be confirmed by cross-examining known Iraqi losses with Iranian claims, none of the Foxbats involved was successfully intercepted: unsurprisingly, the operations of No. 97 Squadron emboldened Saddam Hussein to declare the whole of Iranian airspace to be a 'Military Exclusion Zone' and threatened to intercept international airliner traffic over the country. While largely ignored by the 'hawks' in Tehran, such declarations were taken very seriously – both at home in Iraq, and in the West, and thus the situation became a major propaganda victory for Baghdad.

Sadly, next to no useful photographs of Iraqi MiG-25RBs from the time of the war with Iran are available – which is a particular pity considering IrAF crews accumulated more combat experience with this version than all its other users combined. This is the cockpit section of a MiG-25RB captured by US troops in 2003, and undergoing restoration at Wright Patterson AFB in the USA. Notably, the five-digit serial (25105 in this case) was introduced only in 1989: prior to that, this consisted of four digits. (National Aviation Museum)

Another view of the MiG-25RB 25105 inside a hangar at Wright Patterson. It is seen here without wings and with the right fin disassembled and positioned next to the left engine. Built of nickel-steel, and capable of accelerating to speeds of up to Mach 2.83, the MiG-25 was a big aircraft: almost 24 metres long, it weighed 20,000kg empty and 36,720kg when fully loaded. Its maximum bombload consisted of eight 500kg FAB-500T bombs. (National Aviation Museum)

The left wing of an Iraqi MiG-25RB found in the junkyard of the former Taqaddum AB. Notably, it still had remnants of the MBDZ ejector rack, which could carry two FAB-500Ts mounted in tandem. (Tom Cooper collection)

Another view of the same wreckage, showing the front part of the MBDZ bomb rack. Notable is the position of the national marking, which on the wings of MiG-25RBs were applied inclined outwards. (Tom Cooper collection)

FOXBAT TRAP

Air raids on Tehran prompted a strong Iranian reaction. While the IRGC fired another R-17E at the Ministry of Defence in Baghdad – which missed and hit the building of a major bank, about one kilometre away from the target – the IRIAF redeployed several Grumman F-14A Tomcat interceptors to TFB.1 in Tehran, and its crews flew intensive combat air patrols west of the city. However, because Iraqi MiG-25RB pilots continued making use of the gaps in the Iranian radar network, they were usually detected only when already deep inside Iranian airspace, just minutes away from releasing their bombs. Combined with the limitations of the AWG-9 radar and weapons system – which required the Tomcat to position itself almost directly in front of the incoming MiG-25RB before opening fire – they next to never had the time to intercept with effect. Furthermore, Iraqi Foxbats always remained above and away from the effective engagement altitude of Iranian MIM-23B I-HAWK SAM systems.

In its search for a solution, the personnel of the IRIAF Missile Workshops in Esfahan eventually attempted to adapt longer-ranged RIM-66A Standard SAMs taken from warships of the Iranian Navy to the MIM-23B System. The idea was that the RIM-66A with its ability to reach an altitude of 25,000m (82,000ft), had a better chance of actually scoring a kill than the MIM-23B with its operational ceiling of 20,000m. Therefore, they adapted one of the M192 launchers for I-HAWKs for the use of Standards, and fine-tuned their seeker heads for guidance by the Improved Continuous Wave Acquisition Radar and MPQ-46 High Power Illuminator of the MIM-23B system. The weapon

was deployed in combat for the first time on 4 April 1985, when one RIM-66A detonated about 500 metres behind the MiG-25RB piloted by Captain Mahmoud during his third raid on Tehran. As far as it became known, this was the closest that any Iranian SAM came to an IrAF MiG-25RB during this phase of the wear. With the Standard failing in its new task, the Iranians gave up on the project, and concentrated on attempts to catch one of the Iraqi Foxbats with the help of their manned interceptors. This in turn encouraged the IrAF to send its R-40-armed MiG-25PDSs into Iran, flying the flight profiles of MiG-25RBs. On 21 March 1985, one of the Iraqi Foxbat interceptors shot down a McDonnell Douglas F-4E Phantom II piloted by Major Khalatbari of the IRIAF as it was climbing towards the perceived 'bomber'.

A rare photograph of RIM-66A Standard missiles installed on the M192 launcher of the MIM-23B I-HAWK SAM system of the IRIAF in 1985. Notable is the use of the standard BRU-41 multiple ejector rack (MER) as an adapter between the missile and the launch rail. (Farzin Nadimi collection)

SECOND PHASE

The series of Iranian R-17E strikes on Iraq, and Iraqi air strikes on Iran eventually resulted in what the Iraqi and Western press nicknamed the 'War of the Cities': in Iran, air raids by Iraqi MiG-25RBs became known as the 'Tehran Blitz'. This ended through UN mediation on 6 April 1985, by when the Iraqi armed forces had fired 118 FROG-7 and Scud missiles and flew air raids on 29 targets in Iran. Official Iranian sources blamed Baghdad for attacking civilians only, killing 1,227 and wounding 4,882: however, all targets were actually of military nature. Only the lack of precision of the Soviet technology prevented the Iraqis from hitting their targets more often. In turn, while the Iranians declared the Iraqi Ministry of Defence in Baghdad to be their primary target, most of their missiles never hit that or any other proclaimed target: indeed, many fell in the outskirts of the city, or hit empty spaces inside it, and rarely caused more than a handful of casualties.

When the IRGC fired another R-17E at Baghdad on 26 May 1985, Saddam ordered the IrAF to retaliate with the second phase of the War of the Cities – and this time to widen the targeting list of No. 97 Squadron. Amongst others, its MiG-25RBs now attempted to hit the Iranian Army's Staff College, and several IRGC bases in Tehran. In a total of 105 air and missile strikes launched by 14 June of that year (43 of these by MiG-25RBs against Tehran), the Iraqi armed forces targeted 37 different military facilities. According to Tehran, 570 civilians were killed and 1,332 wounded. Once again, the Iranian means of defence proved insufficient: only once, on 3 June 1985, did IRIAF Tomcats manage to reach a position from which one of them fired an AIM-54A Phoenix missile at one of the MiG-25RBs approaching the Iranian capital. The missile proximity fused too far away and the Iraqi fighter-bomber was only slightly damaged. Ultimately, this First War of the Cities came to an end thanks to another round of intensive, UN mediated negotiations.

8

BITTER YEAR

As is clear from what has already been described, all through 1980–1985, Iraq remained heavily dependent on imported arms systems, or limited to funding the development of new weapons systems abroad. On the contrary, efforts by the MIC to upgrade the capacity of the Iraqi military industries remained limited. Certainly enough, by 1986, another big complex of armament factories was operational at Camp Taji, north of Baghdad, helping make Iraq self-sufficient in regards of small-calibre ammunition, most artillery shells, CBUs, mortar rounds, rocket-propelled grenades and unguided rockets, and two calibres of mortars. Numerous smelters, foundries, and form works were operational, too. However, in grand total, the output of all these works still accounted for less than 2 percent of the total output of the entire economy: similarly, the machinery and transport equipment accounted for only 6 percent of the total output value. For all practical purposes, Iraq still had to import the mass of intermediate components in order to make finished products. Unlikely as it might sound, even at the times of greatest distress – such as during major Iranian offensives – there was never a trace of alarm at the various headquarters in Baghdad. On the contrary, the High Command, the mass of commanders of the Iraqi armed forces, the MIC, and the Iraqi defence sector all went on with business as usual, continuing to be as preoccupied as before with plans for the acquisition of new equipment and development of the force 'after the war'.

Furthermore, with the mass of Iraqi-sponsored research and development projects conducted abroad still incomplete, as of 1986 Iran was still capable of shelling, or at least rocketing, major Iraqi urban centres – primarily Baghdad and Basra – while Iraq still lacked the means to retaliate against major Iranian urban centres.

FROM CAPACITY TO CAPABILITY

By early 1986, Iraqi capabilities with regards to COMINT/ELINT/SIGINT were fully developed, and included the Japanese-made RM-858 HF/DF systems deployed to monitor Iranian communications at the strategic level. However, the GMID remained unable to intercept and decrypt the high frequency troposcatter and microwave communications used by the Iranians to pass their high-level decisions. Thus, on the evening of 9 February 1986, the Iranians took the Iraqis by surprise through launching an amphibious assault on the Faw Peninsula, capturing the town of Faw, and then almost reaching the port of Umm-ol Qassr in the west, and the southern outskirts of Basra in the north. With a single blow, Iraq was effectively cut off from the northern Persian Gulf. Thus began a battle that was to provide the crucial impulse for the ultimate outcome of the entire war – and the high point of the indigenous Iraqi armament industry.[1]

Conducted under the cover of bad weather, the Iranian offensive on Faw caught the Iraqis wrong-footed. Not only had the GMID provided no forewarning, but clouds and rain hampered the IrAF, the redeployment of Iraqi ground forces, and their deployment of chemical weapons in attempts to slow down the enemy advance. As a result, the first series of Iraqi counterattacks was easily repulsed and when reserve forces staged counterattacks, the battle ended in a bloody stalemate that bled both sides white. The Faw Peninsula remained in Iranian hands. The resulting concerns – in Baghdad and within the GCC – were a particularly sobering experience for Saddam, the RCC, the High Command, the GMID and the MIC; indeed, the 'bitter pill' necessary for all of them to *finally* place the conduct of the war into the hands of professional military officers and to intensify the development of their domestic arms industry to unprecedented levels. The result was a series of deep reforms that was to have a profound effect upon the subsequent flow of the war. No other branch of the Iraqi military was to benefit from these as much as the IrAF: Sha'ban and his staff were now given a free hand with regards to planning and conducting operations that were to cause serious – and lasting – economic problems for Tehran and, indeed, to demonstrate not only to the Iraqis and to the international community, but even to the 'hawks' in Tehran, that the IrAF was capable of winning a war.

REORGANISATION OF THE MIC

Under pressure 'to do something', Saddam created a committee presided over by Hussein Kamil, to find a way of rapidly improving the output of the defence sector. Before long, Kamil drew the conclusion that despite six years of war, Iraq's armament factories were still working at a peace-time pace, eight hours a day. Unsurprisingly, their total output was low. For example, the Hiteen Factory was producing about one hundred and fifty 122mm and 130mm artillery shells, or 82mm and 120mm mortar bombs – a month. Kamil promptly issued the order for its director to hire additional workers and to work 24 hours a day, in two shifts of 12 hours. Moreover, he demanded that the Hiteen Factory increase its output to 7,000 mortar bombs and/or artillery shells a month. Immediately after, he rushed to issue similar orders to most other factories, including al-Qadessiya, Saddam, ash-Shaheed, Salahuddin, Nasser, al-Faris, Badr, and Aqaba. Obviously,

A pair of Iraqi Tu-22 supersonic bombers: in 1986–1987, the type was deployed to strike concentrations of Iranian infantry with the heaviest conventional bombs in the Iraqi arsenal. (Tom Cooper collection)

BLINDERS AGAINST ABADAN

The first results of the reorganisation of the MIC were felt by the Iranians during the summer of 1986, when the IrAF began striking IRGC positions on the Faw Peninsula with – amongst others – Tu-22s armed with locally manufactured Nasser bombs. The airspace over the peninsula was heavily protected by Iranian MIM-23B I-HAWK SAM sites deployed on the eastern side of the Shatt al-Arab, outside the range of the Iraqi artillery. In order to avoid suffering heavy losses, the IrAF was forced to carry out almost every single air strike as a complex operation. However, all the investment in the latest French hardware for electronic warfare began paying off under these circumstances. Between 1984 and 1986, France delivered the last of 32 Mirage F.1EQs ordered in 1978 (all arrived upgraded to the F.1EQ-2 standard), and also Mirage F.1EQ-4s ordered in 1981. Moreover, Thomson-CSF had concluded the deliveries of Baz-AR anti-radiation missiles and followed up with Thomson-CSF TMV-004 Caiman broad-band offensive stand-off jammers, and Thomson-CSF TMV-018 Syrel electronic intelligence (ELINT) pods. The combination of all these systems enabled the IrAF to start fighting the air war against Iran in an entirely new fashion – in large formations, heavily protected by aircraft equipped for electronic warfare, custom tailored to counter Iranian I-HAWKs, F-14 Tomcats, and other means of air defence.

Correspondingly, every operation began with one or a pair of Syrel-equipped F.1EQ-2s patrolling at high altitude along the combat zone, monitoring the work of the Iranian air defences – especially the fire-control radars of I-HAWKs – and, via a datalink, 'feeding' the resulting picture to the headquarters of the French-constructed Kari integrated air defence system (IADS) at Muthenna AB in Baghdad. Depending on the Iranian activity, two or four Caiman-equipped Mirage F.1EQ-4s would then approach the target zone to jam the signals of Iranian radars. They would be closely followed by pairs of Mirage F.1EQ-2s armed with Baz-ARs and/or Sukhoi Su-22M-2Ks and Su-22M-3Ks armed with Kh-28 anti-radiation missiles that would target any active Iranian radar stations or the fire-control systems of Iranian I-HAWKs. Immediately after, either a pair or a quartet of Tupolev Tu-16 medium bombers would lay a 'chaff corridor': essentially a form of radar countermeasures in which small, thin pieces of aluminium were spread, that either appeared as a cluster of primary targets or completely swamped the screen of Iranian radars with thousands of fake radar echoes, distracting and confusing the opponent. In this way, the following formations of bomb-armed Mirages, Sukhois and Tu-22s were free to operate along the resulting chaff corridor, without the danger of being engaged by deadly MIM-23Bs. Nassers released by the Tu-22s regularly caused severe losses to the Iranian infantry. In addition to enemy positions on the Faw, the primary targets became concentrations of Iranian troops east of the Shatt al-Arab, mainly in the Abadan area, and their embarkation points along the waterway. By delivering massive blows with Nassers, the Iraqis sought not

an effort of this kind was foremost an issue of logistics: finding the necessary workforce was of crucial importance. With the mass of Iraqi men already serving in the armed forces, there had been a huge lack of workers right from the start of the war. While this was largely solved by employing Egyptians – up to two million of whom worked in Iraq between 1980 and 1988 – this was still not enough. The situation was even more complex considering that the defence sector needed employees with relatively rare skills. Undaunted, Kamil continued pushing and, when the factories failed to meet his objectives, launched a new initiative, in late 1986 – though this time with more realistic aims. For example, the Hiteen Factory was now expected to manufacture 4,000 mortar bombs a month. Although Saddam proved very happy with this plan – making Kamil very proud and even more ambitious – the result was another undershoot: the Hiteen, al-Qa'qaa and al-Qadessiya factories did manage to increase their output, but only to a limited degree. Within 33 days after the start of this campaign, they manufactured only 4,468 mortar bombs in total.

While continuing to exercise immense pressure upon the directors responsible, Kamil meanwhile sought other solutions. Amongst others, in early 1987, he ordered the German-constructed Badr motor vehicle factory to be repurposed for the production of bomb casings based on the French-designed SAMP 400kg Type-21C bomb, and relaunched the production of casings for Soviet-designed FAB-1500M-54s, FAB-3000M-54s, FAB-5000M-54s, and FAB-9000M-54s. The French-designed bombs were then filled with TNT at the Qa'qaa factory, resulting in the bomb with Iraqi designation R-400; the Soviet designs under the designation: Nasser, followed by their weight. Furthermore, Kamil launched a major expansion of the Taji complex: by 1988, this was doubled in size and with help of construction companies from the USSR and Yugoslavia, the factories situated there became capable of producing 1,000 artillery barrels a year, and to carry out overhauls of T-54/55 and T-62 MBTs, and even a limited assembly of T-72s from knock-down kits imported from abroad. That said, Iraq remained heavily reliant on foreign technical support for complex overhauls and repairs of its Czechoslovak, French and Soviet-made aircraft, and this issue was never solved to a satisfactory degree.

only to reduce the enemy pressure, but indeed, to limit – if not to stop – the flow of Iranian reinforcements and supplies over the Shatt al-Arab.

GREAT HARVEST

The tactics of providing heavy electronic warfare support to all strike formations approaching the frontlines between Basra and western Khuzestan proved highly effective and helped greatly decrease the losses of the Iraqi Air Force through 1986. By 1987, the issue of availability of such support became decisive in the 'go' or 'no go' for almost every single operation in this area. If any of the support aircraft was forced to abort because of technical malfunction or other reasons, the entire strike – frequently including up to five or six squadrons of fighter-bombers with 50–70 aircraft – would be cancelled. What happened when the electronic-warfare support did not appear on time and the strike was flown due to a failure to communicate this, was demonstrated on 9 January 1987, during the IRGC's Operation Karbala-5, known as the 'Great Harvest' in Iraq. The fact that the Caiman-equipped Mirages were forced to abort their mission was not communicated to the HQ in Muthenna in time. As a result, the four Tu-16s supposed to deploy chaff flew into the target zone in the Abadan area, did so in full view of Iranian radars at an altitude of 12,200 metres. One of them was shot down by MIM-23Bs with the loss of its entire crew. The importance of

French-made electronic countermeasure systems (ECM) became clear during the following days. On 17 January 1987, Saddam Hussein ordered the IrAF to begin a new round of the War of the Cities. Over the following 42 days, Iraqi fighter-bombers flew 860 combat sorties targeting military facilities in 66 urban centres in western Iran. Because operations deeper into Iran required the involved aircraft to load fuel instead of ECM systems, they found themselves exposed to IRIAF interceptors. As a consequence, the IrAF suffered one of the worst spates of losses in this war – 11 combat aircraft – and the month of February 1987 became known as 'Black February' within its ranks. The consternation was sufficient to prompt the intensification of work on the development of Iraq's first indigenous ballistic missile.[2]

PROJECT 144

The loss of Faw in February 1986 caused Saddam to grow impatient with the slow progress of Project 395. Therefore, in February 1986 he ordered the MIC to find a way to stretch the range of the Soviet-made R-17E missile to 650km – exactly enough to reach Tehran when fired from within Iraq. Kamil formed the Surface-to-Surface Missile Research and Development Committee (SSMRD), led by rocket scientist Lieutenant General Amer Hammud as-Saadi (educated in Germany, and with experience from working at the Yarmouk factory) and a group of seasoned engineers and officers

from Brigade 224, including (those who are safe to be named in public) Ra'ad Ismail Jamil, and Hassam Hamid Amin. The committee was subjected to the control of the Secretary of the Presidency, Hamid Yusuf Hammadi, who in turn placed the resulting Project 144 under Saddam's direct auspices – and outside the chain-of-command of the Ministry of Defence.

Working in offices adjacent to the home base of Brigade 224, in Camp Taji, Saadi and his team approached their task in methodical fashion. The first issue was to define how each part of the R-17E worked, in order to find out how its performance could be modified. After less than a handful of meetings, the conclusion was that the only way to stretch the range was to increase the size of the two fuel tanks. Calculations showed that the tank for the IRFNA had to be stretched by 45cm, and the tank for the kerosene by 87cm.

Once all the studies were completed, in mid-1987 the team had one of Brigade 224's R-17Es brought to its workshop and fixed atop two railway flatcars: the idea was that when they cut it into two, each part

The wreckage of a French-made SAMP Type 21C 400kg bomb that failed to detonate. This weapon was manufactured under licence in Iraq under the designation R-400. (Farzin Nadimi collection)

A stock of R-400 bombs found by US troops in 1991. (US DoD)

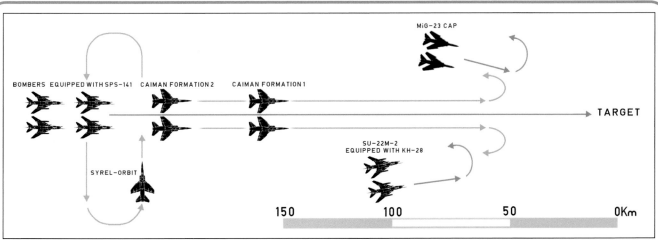

A diagram showing a typical Iraqi Close Air Support or Battlefield Aerial Interdiction operation as undertaken from February–March 1984 until the end of the war:

- 1 F.1EQ-2 equipped with the Syrel pod would monitor the activity of the Iranian air defences from a stand-off range;
- 2–4 Mirages equipped with Caiman pods and in a column formation, with four minutes of separation between the two elements, would enter the combat zone about 150 kilometres from the nearest HAWK site at an altitude of 10,700m and speed of 1,100km/h; they would activate their pods and continue approaching until about 50 kilometres from the SAM site;
- The Caiman-equipped Mirages would be accompanied by 1–3 Su-22M-2Ks equipped with Myetel pods and Kh-28s, which would operate in a racetrack pattern about 60km from the nearest known HAWK SAM site;
- 2–4 MiG-23MFs flew a combat air patrol;
- If involved, Tu-16 and Tu-22 bombers would deploy a combination of noise and repeater jammers, and chaff, while formations of fighter-bombers were led by examples either equipped with internally installed SPS-141s (MiG-23BNs), or pod-mounted SPS-141s (Su-22s), or Mirages equipped with Remora pods.

The Iranian-operated MIM-23B I-HAWK SAM system was generally considered the most dangerous opponent of the IrAF, and grudgingly nicknamed 'Death Valley' by its pilots. (Farzin Nadimi collection)

Part of the electronic warfare arsenal developed by the French in response to orders from Iraq, and with the help of Iraqi funding, from left to right: Thomson-CSF TMV-002 Remora pod, two pairs of Thomson-CSF TMV-004 Caiman pods, and a pair of Matra Sycomor chaff and flare dispensers (nearest to the camera and still partially in their transport containers). (US DoD)

Deployed similarly for close air support, battlefield interdiction, anti-ship and for long-range operations against strategic targets deep within Iran, this combination proved overwhelming to the Iranian air defences: reportedly, it not only caused the radar displays of F-4Es to turn white, or blocked the acquisition and illumination radars of HAWK SAM sites, but caused problems even for the AWG-9s of Iranian F-14s.[3] (Diagram by Tom Cooper)

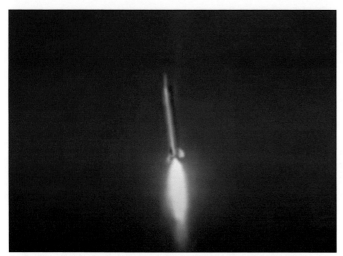

An R-17E ballistic missile seen seconds after its launch by Brigade 224. Characteristic of this liquid-fuelled weapon is its orange trail of flame; a result of burning IRFNA fuel. (Tom Cooper collection)

would remain fixed to one of the wagons, enabling them to apply modifications before bringing the two cars and thus the two parts of the missile together again. To accelerate the entire procedure, the team eventually had eight flatcars and four missiles brought to its workshop.

The next issue was that of what tool to use for cutting? The answer was found through requesting help from the Oil Ministry. The latter sent an engineer – an aged technician who used to work on the installation of pipelines back in the 1950s – together with a suitable cutting machine. However, during the first attempt the fuel tank of one R-17E was completely destroyed. The old engineer decided to try again, but with a different direction of rotation of the saw. This time, the tank was cut without any kind of problems: the engineer was congratulated and – because the entire 'operation' was a top-secret affair – sent away. Having no replacement materials on hand, the team used the 'modified' machine to cut another R-17E into two: the reason was that they needed parts from its fuel tanks to stretch the tanks of the first missile.

The next problem was that of welding the resulting extensions into place: this had to be undertaken with extreme precision, as a deviation of more than 2mm would cause an explosion of the missile on lift-off. The task of finding a welding machine suitable for stainless steel, and of the needed Aragon gas and suitable welding wires nearly caused a big delay in Project 144: it took days to find exactly what the team needed – and then it was found on a construction site in Baghdad where an Indian company was involved.

Once everything was finally in place, Saadi's team welded all the pieces together, thus creating a new, 132cm longer and – when fully fuelled – 859kg heavier version of the R-17E, named al-Hussein.

INITIAL TESTING

While successful, the extension in length and increased weight of al-Hussein only caused additional problems: not only was the carrier arm of the MAZ-543 TEL much too short, but the battery powering the missile guidance system was originally designed to supply only enough energy for a flight time of 60 seconds. The added 21 seconds of flight time of the new missile not only exhausted the battery: testing on the ground revealed that when al-Hussein was fired to its maximum range, 650km, its motor tended to burn cables connecting the guidance system with steering nozzles at the base of the missile. Such experiences proved crucial for the success of Project 144, for they forced the Iraqis to find solutions that were both dependable and worked.

Once the first prototype of the al-Hussein missile was ready Saadi's team was keen to run a test flight. This was organised in July 1987 at a test launch site near al-Wallid Air Base (formerly H-3 airfield) in western Iraq, aiming for an area south of the town of an-Nasiriya. The missile fired and lifted off as planned but exploded after only 12 seconds. Subsequent investigation revealed that the new weapon required a modified mechanical timer to operate the circuitry for nozzles and valves. Suitable adaptations were made by employees of the Badr factory on the second prototype, which also had 20cm longer fins because the team expected that longer fins would improve the stability of the weapon. Moreover, instead of its usual, high-explosive warhead, the Iraqis installed a warhead made of concrete, to be better able to study the wreckage after its landing.

The second prototype of al-Hussein was test launched on 2 August 1987 and flew over 615km. However, on re-entry into Earth's atmosphere, it flipped out of control and fell with its body in a horizontal position – and thus at a relatively slow speed – about four kilometres away from the actual target. Subsequent inspection revealed that the missile landed almost intact, except that its stretched fins were badly burned. The reason was that on its ascent it reached up to 160km altitude – nearly double the maximum apogee of the R-17E at 87km. Thus, it left Earth's atmosphere, and was exposed to high temperatures when re-entering it. While understanding that they had to find a solution for this problem, not only Saadi and his team, but also their supervisor were all highly satisfied.[4]

IMPROVEMENTS

After the first two tests, Saadi decided to make three additional prototypes following the experience with the first two and conduct three additional test flights. Undertaken in October 1987, these included missiles without warheads, to reduce the damage from collision with the ground. In all three tests, the Iraqis experienced the same problems as with the second prototype: the missile came down with its body in the horizontal position, very slowly, about 4,000 metres away from the target. Following extensive investigation, Saadi's team concluded that the missile fell horizontally because additional weight moved its centre of gravity closer to the centre of the fuselage, instead of leaving it where it was: near the warhead. To change this required significant redistribution of the equipment inside the missile, including most of the cabling and piping. Furthermore, the decision was taken to retain the original fins, and not to stretch these by 20cm, in order to lessen the weight.

While the related work was going on, on 13 October 1987, an R-17E fired by the IRGC's Khatam al-Anbya Missile Force hit a school in Baghdad, killing dozens of children. Until that time, Iraq had retaliated to such attacks with air strikes on Iranian urban centres, but this appeared not enough: the Iraqi public began openly questioning why Iraq was not using the same methods to hit back against the Iranians. Saadi's team was now under urgent pressure to deliver. A new round of three test firings was undertaken in November 1987, always with the same result: the missile came down in the horizontal position. The sole difference was that this time the bodies hit the ground about 3,000 metres form the target, while the warheads fell off and landed 4,000 metres away.

The team held a series of conferences to try to figure out the reason, and came out with two possible solutions: one was to apply thermal insulation to the fins; the second to change the centre of gravity once again. As a result, two additional prototypes were prepared, each according to ideas from one part of the team: the second of the two incorporated a major reshuffling of five air bottles from the rear of the missile, to near the warhead, and a reduction of

An R-17E of Brigade 224 – seen during testing related to Project al-Hussein – positioned on its pedestal, on the rear end of a MAZ-543 TEL. (Ali Tobchi collection)

One of the first al-Husseins, seen in the process of being erected by an indigenous Iraqi TEL, installed on the flatbed of a commercial 13.60 tilt-trailer. (Ali Tobchi collection)

the weight of the latter from 1,000kg of TNT to 350kg of RDX (the latter created more overpressure and was thus considered suitable compensation for the loss of weight). Both prototypes were test launched, and the second achieved an excellent result: it entered the Earth's atmosphere while remaining stable, and the warhead hit the ground while flying almost vertically. However, investigation of the wreckage revealed that due to a rupture in the fuel tank caused by the stress of the high-speed descent, the rear part of the missile – including the engine – separated and, once again, hit the ground about 3,000 metres away from the target.

Considering the latter fact not to be a problem, Saadi was satisfied with the result and reported correspondingly to his superiors. In turn, the decision was taken to adapt the second configuration – with air bottles installed near the warhead of reduced size – for series production. The decision was confirmed by another test launch, undertaken on 30 December 1987, with exactly the same result.

SERIES PRODUCTION

Large scale conversion of R-17Es into al-Husseins was initiated at the al-Mustafa factory. The initial rate was at two missiles a week, but this gradually increased, and by 1 January 1988 a total of 42 missiles were ready – as was the first modified MAZ-542 – even if all needed additional work, mainly in downsizing their warheads and redistribution of the five air bottles to the forward part of the fuselage. Through January, two additional workshops joined production, and by 27 February 1988, another 24 missiles were converted.

On that day, Mirage F.1EQs of the IrAF flew a spectacular air strike that ruined much of the Rey Oil Refinery south of Tehran. Together with several other air raids on oil refineries, this caused such a critical shortage of fuel in Iran that the end of the war was actually predetermined: caught with the mass of its troops redeployed to the northern frontlines to Iraq, the IRGC was to prove unable to return these to the crucial southern battlefields for months after. Whether the government in Tehran was aware of these facts remains unclear: what is certain is that it ordered the IRGC's Khatam al-Anbya Missile Force to conduct new strikes on Iraq and Baghdad was hit by three R-17Es. As far as is known, the Iraqi leadership was unaware of the terminal damage IrAF air raids had caused to the Iranian oil industry: whatever the case, Saddam Hussein ordered all-out retaliation. The same afternoon and evening, Missile Brigade 224 fired nine al-Husseins at Tehran. Thus began the Second War of the Cities.

THE SECOND WAR OF THE CITIES

Back in November 1987 the officers of Missile Brigade 224 had pre-selected three launching sites for al-Husseins:

- outside the town of Sulaymaniyah, in north-eastern Iraq
- near Jalawla, about 200km north-east of Baghdad
- al-Fakkah, 300km south-east of Baghdad and north of the Howeizeh Marshes

The use of the first site was soon out of question because Sulaymaniyah was traditionally a hotbed of armed Kurdish resistance. Jalawla appeared as a good alternative and the first modified MAZ-543 was sent there in December – only to run into an ambush set up by the Kurds, from which the crew barely managed to extricate their precious vehicle without serious damage. Therefore, the commanding officer of Missile Brigade 224 was left with little choice but to use al-Fakkah. From this site, on 28 and 29 February

The site of a hit by an al-Hussein missile in downtown Tehran in late February 1988. While not really decisive in the outcome of the Iran–Iraq War, the Iraqi capability to hit the Iranian capital several times a day left the population in a state of shock, and war weary. (via Ali Tobchi)

1988 the unit fired 16 or 17 al-Husseins at Tehran. Such a massive blow shocked the Iranians, prompting their government to publish reports of Iraq receiving Soviet-made Tupolev Tu-22K supersonic bombers armed with hypersonic Kh-22 cruise missiles (a report that caused quite some alarm within US intelligence circles). And yet, this was only the start. The IRGC did 'retaliate', firing a total of total of 23 R-17Es (or their North Korean-made copies, the Hwasong-5) at Baghdad by 10 March 1988. However, not only had the Iranians thus completely exhausted their stocks of ballistic missiles, but the Iraqis rocketed Tehran, Rasht, Qorveh, Shiraz, Hamedan, Zanjan, and the holy city of Qom with a total of 68 additional al-Husseins within the same timeframe. Iraq thus emerged as a clear-cut winner of this campaign.

The reignited War of the Cities then experienced a few days of break, as both sides became preoccupied with Iran's final large-scale offensive into Iraq, this time undertaken on the northern frontlines. On the night of 13 to 14 March 1988, the IRGC unleashed nine of its infantry divisions, supported by one division of the regular Iranian Army, and nine independent brigades – a total of 130,000 troops – in Operation Valfajr-10. The plan was to overrun the town of Halabja (also 'Halabcheh'), secure the strategically important Daraband-i-Khan Dam, and then press in a western direction deep into Iraq. Although forewarned, the High Command in Baghdad was still taken by surprise: consequently, by 15 March, the IRGC and allied Kurds – supported by 90 air strikes by the IRIAF and nearly 600 sorties by combat helicopters of the Islamic Republic of Iran Army Aviation – secured the town of Halabja, and then continued in the direction of the lake of Darband-i-Khan. Facing this onslaught, the 43rd Infantry Division of the Iraqi Army fell apart: it suffered over 4,000 casualties, had its headquarters overrun and its commander (Brigadier General Ali al-Alkawi) captured, and lost over 200 armoured fighting vehicles. Baghdad ordered the two divisions deployed north and south of the Iranian penetration to hold their positions high in the mountains at any cost, while rushing all the available reinforcements – equivalent to an entire mechanised corps – into the battle. The IrAF flew about 100 combat sorties every day,

in addition to a similar number by attack helicopters of the Iraqi Army Aviation Corps. When all of this showed next to no effect, Iraq deployed chemical weapons, killing thousands. The Iranian advance was stopped and all subsequent attempts to break through the Iraqi frontlines at other points were beaten back: the Iranian offensive petered out by 19 April 1988. For all practical purposes, Tehran had run out options to conclude the war successfully.

LIBERATION OF FAW

The Iranian offensive on the northern battlefields was still in full swing when Iraq prepared a series of counteroffensives aimed at reducing the IRGC to the point where Iran could not continue fighting the war. The most important of such operations was the liberation of the Faw Peninsula, held by Iranians since February 1986. Because all Iraqi counteroffensives with this aim had failed in 1986 and 1987, Baghdad expected fierce Iranian resistance and was thus determined not to leave anything to fate.

One of the most important issues was the need to knock out the large pontoon bridge that the Iranians had constructed across the Shatt al-Arab waterway to the southern Faw Peninsula. Imported from North Korea, this was kept afloat by a combination of steel pipes and large blocks of Styrofoam: it not only proved exceptionally hard to knock out even with direct hits from heavy bombs and ballistic missiles, but was also well protected, including one site each of HAWKs and British-made Rapier SAMs, several teams operating man-portable air defence systems, and about two dozen anti-aircraft guns. Through 1987, the IrAF attempted to hit it several times, mainly with its brand-new Su-22M-4s, equipped with Kh-25L (ASCC/NATO codename 'AS-10 Karen') and Kh-29L ('AS-14 Kedge') laser-guided missiles. However, this combination suffered a major drawback: upon releasing the missile the pilot had to continue moving in the direction of the target, carefully keeping his visor pointed at the target until the weapon's impact because the laser-marker was installed in the nose cone of the Su-22M-4 and fixed in all axes. As result, the aircraft flew straight and into the middle of the envelope of all the Iranian anti-aircraft weapons, which caused the

The Avibrás SS-30 Artillery Saturation Rocket System (Astros) was developed to Iraqi specifications in the late 1970s and early 1980s. The primary weapons were 127mm rockets with a range of 30km, 32 of which were carried by each launcher. The launchers were 7m long, 2.9m high and 2.9m wide, lightly armoured against small arms fire, and weighed 10,000kg. Iraq acquired a total of 11 batteries with 66 Astros II Mk 3 launchers. Other vehicles in a battery included a command/mobile weather station vehicle, one fire-control vehicle, six launchers, six vehicles carrying reloads, and one mobile workshop, with all vehicles painted in a cardboard-like colour overall. They were deployed extensively during the war with Iran, from 1982 until 1988. (Artwork by David Bocquelet)

An LRSV-232 launcher of the M-87 Orkan/Ababil-50 multiple rocket launch system, jointly developed by Yugoslavia and Iraq in the mid-1980s. The primary weapons were 262mm R-262 rockets with a range of 50km. The launcher was 9m long, 2.64m wide and 3.84m tall, and weighed about 15,000kg. Much simpler than the Astros II, the system used the precise alignment of the launcher, and high-quality tubes to attain the necessary precision and range, and every launcher was equipped with its own crane for quick reloading. Each battery included four LRSV-232 launchers, four trucks carrying reloads, one command vehicle, two topographic survey vehicles, two observation vehicles and two meteorological vehicles. In addition to a single prototype, Iraq received only one battery of Ababil-50s, but because of the high quality of their ammunition and simplicity of their launchers, they played an important role in the further development of indigenous weapons systems. (Artwork by David Bocquelet)

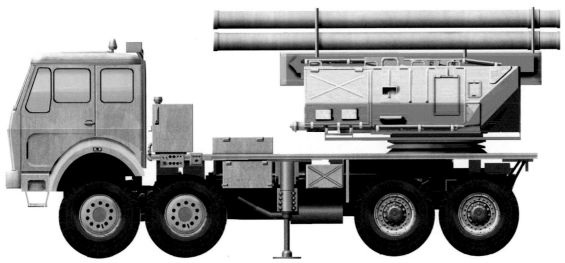

In 2000–2001, under Project Ababil-100, the Iraqis increased the number of launchers for Ababil-50 rockets by installing the SM-90 launcher of the S-75/SA-2 SAM system onto the flatbed of FAP 3232 trucks originally used to carry reloads for the Ababil-50. The number of tubes was decreased to six per launcher, and tubes were installed on a shortened arm from the SM-90. The resulting Ababil-50/Dvina was put on display during a military parade in Baghdad, but it remains unclear if any saw action during the US invasion of 2003. (Artwork by David Bocquelet)

The same combination of FAP 3232 trucks and SM-90 launchers (though with the arms of their launchers retaining most of their full length) served as the mount for Ababil-100/Fath rockets, which saw relatively intensive combat deployment in 2003. Two trucks were modified in this fashion. The Ababil-100/al-Fath (or 'al-Fatah') was a solid-propelled, short-range ballistic missile, with a length of 6.7m, and diameter of 0.5m. It weighed 1,200kg on launch and could deliver a warhead of 260–300kg (the same as that of the Samoud II missile) over a range of more than 100km. One Ababil-100/Fath scored a direct hit on the HQ of the 2nd Brigade of the 3rd Infantry Division, US Army, on 7 April 2003, killing five and injuring at least 14 personnel. A submunition warhead filled with KB-1 bomblets from the M-87 Orkan/Ababil-50 system using a barometric fuse was never developed to full satisfaction and, apparently, never deployed in combat. (Artwork by David Bocquelet)

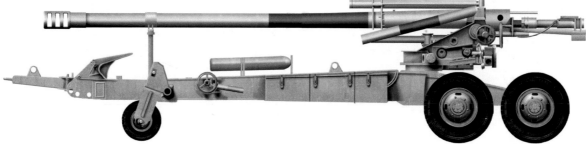

Iraq's relationship with Gerald Bull's gun designs began in the early 1980s, when the MIC placed an order for 300 GHN-45 howitzers from Austria and 41,000 155mm shells from Belgium. Deliveries began in 1984 and ran through to 1985, when cancelled by the MIC. Iraq then placed an order for 250 very similar, but motorised G-5 guns in South Africa under Project Sheri instead. By this time, at least 110 GHN-45s were in Iraq and they saw intensive service during the war with Iran. By August 1990, a similar number of G-5s, which fired the same ammunition, had been imported. Both types of guns saw action during the war of 1991, when they proved less effective than anticipated – primarily because US and Coalition air strikes completely disrupted the Iraqi command and control capabilities, and many were knocked out by fire from M270 MLRS of the US Army. A single GHN-45 weighed about 9,000kg and was about 9.5m long when prepared for transport, as shown here. (Artwork by David Bocquelet)

In 1988, South Africa attempted to sell the G-6 to Iraq. Hussein Kamil liked the design but found it too expensive and requested that Bull design two equivalents for Iraq. Named al-Faw (shown here), and al-Majnoon, these were to carry 210mm and 155mm guns, respectively. The prototype al-Faw was constructed around three 11-metre-long (53 calibres) 210mm guns made by Creusot-Loire of France, and mounted on a custom-made vehicle manufactured by the Spanish company Trabelan (earning it the nickname the 'Spanish Project' amongst the Iraqis involved), powered by a 550hp Mercedes-Benz engine. The complete vehicle was to weigh about 44,000kg but still be able to reach top road speeds of 90km/h. It was to be capable of firing 109.4kg shells over a maximum range of 57km – thus outranging all contemporary US- and Soviet-made artillery. Production was to be carried out by the factories of the Taji complex, but never materialised. (Artwork by David Bocquelet)

The Iraqi contract for Bull's ultimate gun design resulted in Project Babylon: a 1,000mm calibre gun, designed to launch satellites into the Earth's orbit. While most of the required parts – weighing about 1,665 tons in total – were manufactured in Great Britain, France, Belgium and a few other countries, and collected by Iraq, the Babylon Gun was never assembled. Shown here is its 'prototype', named the 'Baby Babylon' by Bull, which was not only assembled but regularly test-fired as of spring 1989. With a 46-metre-long barrel of 350mm calibre, and weighing about 113 tonnes, it had to be constructed on a mountainside at Jebel Hamryin, in the vicinity of the Saad-16 complex, to achieve the desired elevation of 45 degrees. It proved capable of firing metal slugs at speeds of 3,000 metres per second but served no direct military purpose. (Artwork by Anderson Subtil)

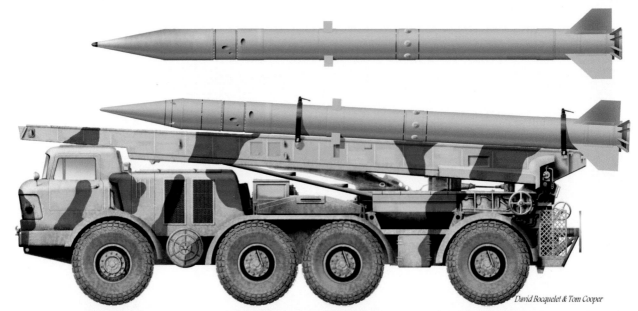

Iraq acquired only eight 9P113 TELs of the 9K52 Luna-9M/FROG-7 system and 9M21 rockets, but they played their role in the development of derivative weapons, foremost the Laith-90 rocket: an extended range 9M21 deployed in numbers during the wars of 1991 and 2003. Early during their service in Iraq, 9P113s were painted in sand overall, and had wide splotches of blue-green, as used on most Iraqi Army vehicles of the late 1970s and early 1980s. By 1991, most were repainted in a darker sand colour with a strong touch of grey. This colour was retained until 2003, by when the SSMD and Brigade 225 was operationally subordinated to the Republican Guards and all had a small red triangle on the doors of the driver's cab. (Artworks by David Bocquelet & Tom Cooper)

The Minski Avtomobilniy Zavod MAZ-543 was an 8x8 cargo vehicle developed in the early 1960s, most famous for serving as a TEL for ballistic missile systems. Depending on the variant, it was between 10.81m and 11.657m long, 3m wide and 2.9m tall, and could haul loads between 19,100kg and 23,000kg. Between 1974 and 1980 Iraq acquired 10 MAZ-543/9P117 TELs and they saw intensive deployment during the war with Iran. All served with Brigade 224, and all were painted in a cardboard-sand colour overall. Some received hull-numbers and small Iraqi flags, as shown here. From 1988, they were used to fire al-Hussein missiles at Iran, nearly all from a site outside al-Fakkah, 300km south-east of Baghdad. R-17Es delivered to Iraq were originally painted in dark green overall, as standard for all Soviet military vehicles. In the early 1980s, the Iraqis started repainting them in various shades of yellow sand. (Artworks by David Bocquelet and Tom Cooper)

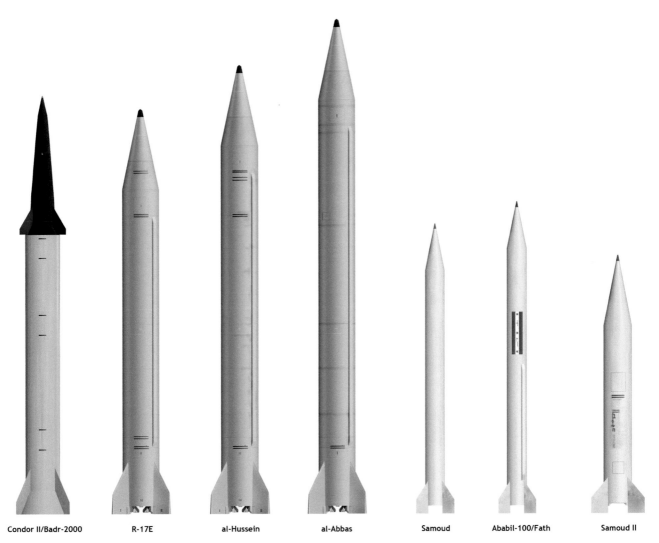

| Condor II/Badr-2000 | R-17E | al-Hussein | al-Abbas | Samoud | Ababil-100/Fath | Samoud II |

Various ballistic missiles developed by Iraq, or on order from Iraq, and that reached at least the state of flight testing are shown here, including (from left to right), Condor II/Badr-2000, R-17E, al-Hussein, al-Abbas, Samoud, Ababil-100/Fath, and Samoud II. (Artworks by Tom Cooper)

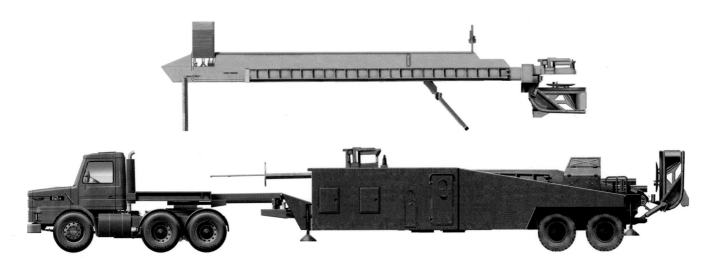

As of 1988–1990, Iraq had developed several types of experimental launchers for R-17E missiles and their indigenous derivatives, two of which entered service. The main artwork shows the TEL developed in 1989 by engineer Wallid Alawi and designated, accordingly, al-Wallid. Towed by a Scania truck, this was constructed on a commercial trailer and contained a locally manufactured, reverse-engineered version of the raising arm from the MAZ-543/9P117 TEL, and a cabin with control panels for the missile. Six such TELs were manufactured in total. The upper artwork shows the final version of the fixed launcher, a total of 56 of which were manufactured, and 28 of which were brought into position in western Iraq between air bases H-2 and H-3 in 1990. (Artworks by David Bocquelet)

The MiG-21 fighter jet was the most common aircraft in the IrAF and flew over 50 percent of combat sorties launched during the war with Iran. Unsurprisingly, the type attracted a number of attempts at modification. The best-known was the installation of French Matra R.550 Magic Mk. I infrared homing air-to-air missiles (made easier by these being compatible with installations for Soviet-made R-13Ms), and a test-installation of the YakB four-barrel 12.7mm machine gun instead of the usual GSh-23 twin-barrel 23mm cannon. In 1990, there were attempts to develop a remotely piloted variant, and in the 2000s, the IrAF experimented with a single MiG-21 the left side of which was painted in radar-absorbent colour. In 1986, four MiG-21bis were painted as shown here for 'naval operations' against IRGC-operated boats and barges on the Shatt al-Arab. (Artwork by Tom Cooper)

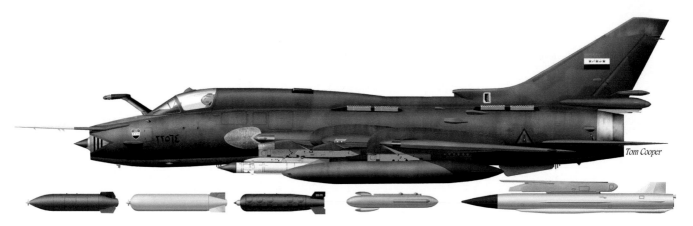

The second most-widely deployed fighter-bomber operated by the IrAF was the Sukhoi Su-20/22-family. Starting in 1981, several Su-22Ms were upgraded through compatibility with Kh-28 anti-radiation missiles (AS-9 Kyle; lower right corner), to the standard locally designated Su-22M-2K. Through the 1980s, they were equipped with (inset, from left to right) two variants of the Cardoen CB.500 and South African SCB.470 CBUs; the large and powerful jets of this family could carry six of each at once. Soviet-made SPG-141E ECM pods (centre bottom inset) became available from around 1984 and proved highly effective. Finally, by 1990, at least two Su-22M-4s were modified by the Iraqis through the addition of French-made IFR probes – the main artwork shows the example with serial number 22564; the other known example was 22481 – and adapted to deploy Kh-25MP anti-radiation missiles (ASCC/NATO codename AS-10 Karen; shown installed on the inboard underwing pylon). (Artwork by Tom Cooper)

The final two years of the war with Iran and the immediate aftermath saw a large number of foreign arms projects to Iraqi specification being finalised, and at least as many indigenous Iraqi arms projects being launched. One of the former reached Iraq in early 1987, in the form of a Dassault Falcon 50 business jet modified through the installation of the avionics and cockpit of a Mirage F.1EQ-5, and the capability to carry and deploy two AM.39 Exocet anti-ship missiles, as shown in the main image. Originally meant to serve as a training tool, and nicknamed 'Suzanna', the jet was used in the strike on the guided-missile frigate USS *Stark* on 17 May of the same year. By 1989, it had received further modifications, including an additional fuel tank installed inside the cabin, and the capability to carry the Raphael TH reconnaissance pod (shown in the lower right corner). Unsurprisingly, Suzanna was taken extremely seriously by the US Navy, prompting it to fly combat air patrols 24/7 over its aircraft carriers in the Red Sea and the Persian Gulf during Operation Desert Shield in the second half of 1990. (Artwork by Tom Cooper)

After testing and combat deployment of PDL-CT-equipped Mirage F.1EQ-5s, serving as target-markers, and Su-22M-3K/M-4s as bombers delivering Soviet-made Kh-29L laser-guided bombs to knock out several Iranian pontoon bridges in April–May 1988, the Iraqis arrived at a new idea. The result was an attempt to install Kh-29 PGMs on their Mirages. Only one aircraft – serial number 4563 – was modified this way, but the adaptation proved quite cumbersome, necessitating the development and installation of an adapter between the French-made Alkan 951B inboard underwing pylon and the Soviet-made APU-58 launch rail for Kh-29Ls. This project was not applied fleet-wide, even if proudly presented in public during the May 1989 arms fair in Baghdad. Shown in the lower left corner is the French-made Baz-AR, developed to Iraqi specifications. (Artwork by Tom Cooper)

Another project from the final months of the war with Iran was less sophisticated: it saw the reworking of all the remaining stocks of R-3S and R-3R air-to-air missiles; their guidance sections were removed and a 130mm artillery shell installed instead. Such weapons were deployed as heavy unguided rockets by Mi-8 helicopters of the Iraqi Army Aviation Corps and their range of more than 2,000 metres enabled them to target Iranian anti-aircraft positions with relative precision, yet without entering the range of enemy air defences. As far as is known, helicopter crews of the IrAAC used BD3-60-21 launch rails to mount R-3S/R missiles on their helicopters. (Artwork by Tom Cooper)

The number of R-3S and R-3R missiles still in the stocks of the IrAF as of 1987–1988 was sufficient to adapt several BMP-1 infantry fighting vehicles for their carriage. The turret with the gun and machine gun was removed and replaced with a pedestal carrying six launch rails for R-3 missiles. As far as is known, all of the modified missiles had been expended by May 1988, and thus the Iraqis rushed to convert their stocks of even older RS-2U air-to-air missiles to a similar configuration. This project was completed only after the armistice with Iran. (Artworks by David Bocquelet and Tom Cooper)

The MIC's efforts to acquire what was to become its most advanced combat aircraft ever culminated in a contract for 60 Dassault Mirage 2000 two-seat strike-fighters signed on 16 February 1982 (together with the order for Mirage F.1EQ-4s). It prompted – and financed – the development of an entirely new generation of avionic systems and weapons, like the Antelope radar and fire-control system, an advanced targeting pod similar to what eventually became the Atlis II, the MICA air-to-air missile (shown as installed on the outboard underwing pylon), and a conventional version of the ASAMP supersonic land-attack missile. This order never materialised, but a new contract for 54 Mirage 2000s was signed in 1989, when a model in the camouflage colours shown here was put on a display at the Baghdad arms fair. That contract was cancelled in the aftermath of the UN-imposed arms embargo of August 1990. (Artwork by Tom Cooper)

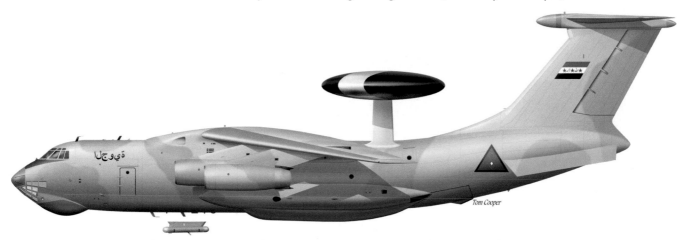

Iraq's efforts to obtain an AEW or AWACS aircraft were centred on two primary components: a Tigre-G radar of French origin manufactured under licence by the Saad-16 Works, and the Soviet-made Ilyushin Il-76 transport. In 1989–1990, this effort resulted in the emergence of the first two viable platforms. The Adnan-1 (always painted in white on the top fuselage and light grey elsewhere) was the first to have its radar installed in a radome atop a twin-arm pedestal above the rear fuselage. Adnan-2, which wore a camouflage pattern in two shades of grey, as reconstructed here, was much more advanced and, as of late 1990, approaching the level of development short of entering operational service. Notably, both could carry the Thomson-CSF TMV-018 Syrel ESM-pod under the central fuselage (shown inset). Their further development ended on 16 January 1991, when the Adnan-2 was destroyed by US laser-guided bombs while parked at Taqaddum AB, while Adnan-1 was evacuated to Iran a few weeks later. (Artwork by Tom Cooper)

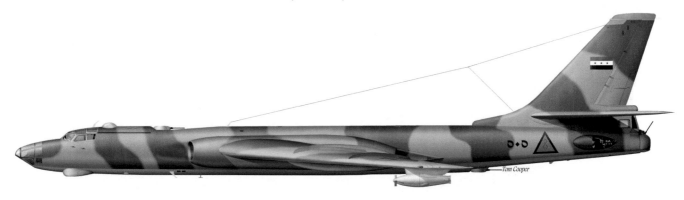

Another long-standing IrAF requirement was that for a tanker aircraft. The first related conversion took place in 1983 and consisted of parking and securing a fuel truck inside the cargo hold of an Il-76MD, and connecting it to a Douglas/Intertechnique D-704 refuelling pod installed underneath the rear cargo door. This solution was abandoned in favour of using Mirage F.1EQ-4s and F.1EQ-5s as buddy-tankers during the last three years of the war with Iran, because of their superior survivability. Immediately after the ceasefire, the MIC then initiated a project of converting old Tupolev Tu-16 bombers into tankers. Details of this project remain scarce, but at least one aircraft – serial number 505 – was modified through the installation of one D-704 pod under each wingtip. This was also flight tested in 1989–1990, but never deployed operationally. This artwork is a reconstruction of the left profile of the Tu-16 in question, based on the only piece of visual evidence available: a mural that decorated one of the squadron ready-rooms at Saddam AB. (Artwork by Tom Cooper)

In late 1990, rising tensions with the US-led Coalition prompted the IrAF to search for ways to improve the survivability of its MiG-23ML fleet. Correspondingly, several MiG-23MLs of No. 93 Squadron were equipped to carry Thomson-CSF TMV-002 Remora ECM pods. Furthermore, their avionics were enhanced through the installation of the SPO-15 radar warning systems on the fin, and ASO-2 chaff and flare dispensers on the top central fuselage. While the Remora proved effective against Iranian interceptors of the late 1980s, by 1991 it was no secret to the Western powers. Nevertheless, aircraft equipped in this fashion caused quite some confusion amongst US fliers in January 1991, when at least two were claimed shot down as 'Mirage F.1EQ' – obviously on basis of intelligence data only. (Artwork by Tom Cooper)

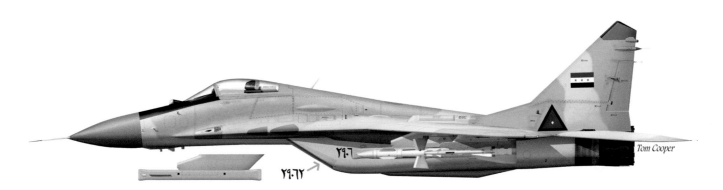

After upgrading MiG-23MLs, the MIC launched similar works on at least two MiG-29 (9.12B) of No. 6 Squadron (serials 29040 and 29062). Both received additional piping, which made their inboard underwing hardpoints capable of carrying drop tanks. Both could carry TMV-002 Remora ECM pods on the same stations. In turn, large launch rails for R-27R medium range, semi-active radar homing missiles (ASCC/NATO codename 'AA-10 Alamo'), were moved to the central underwing station. Outboard stations remained occupied by launchers for short-range R-60 air-to-air missiles. Notably, Iraq never received any R-27Ts (the infrared homing variant of the 'AA-10 Alamo'), nor any R-73s (ASCC/NATO codename 'AA-11 Archer'). Both 29040 and 29062 survived the war of 1991, but the entire fleet was grounded by 1995 for the lack of resources. (Artwork by Tom Cooper)

Perhaps the most promising Iraqi project related to developing an anti-AWACS capability was launched in 1998, when the MIC and the IrAF decided to modify one of the surviving MiG-25RB reconnaissance/strike-fighters through the installation of a Fantasmagoria anti-radiation targeting pod and Kh-58 anti-radiation missiles. For unknown reasons, the work never proceeded beyond stripping down the aircraft in question. Details about its serial remain unknown, but this reconstruction shows one of the last two MiG-25RBs delivered to Iraq, as it would probably have looked once ready and equipped with an underwing hardpoint from a MiG-25PD interceptor, carrying the APU-58 launch rail necessary for deployment of the Kh-58 missile. It is likely that the installation of the Fantasmagoria would have required the installation of additional aerials on the nose, but exact details of these remain unknown. (Artwork by Tom Cooper)

The final project involving the IrAF prior to the US-led invasion of 2003, envisaged the conversion of Aero L-29 Delfin two-seat jet trainers into remotely piloted aircraft. Initiated in 1997 at the Ibn Firnas Centre by a team led by Dr. Mahmoud Modhaffer, this effort included the installation of a control system taken from the Italian-made Mirach-100 target-UAV, an autopilot and four cameras. The first test flight was undertaken on 13 April 1997, but was not successful; the second was more fruitful, but in August of the same year the modified L-29 crashed 60–70km southeast of Mutasim AB. Further development was interrupted by Operation Desert Fox in December 1998 and then cancelled after another crash in spring 2001. (Artwork by Tom Cooper)

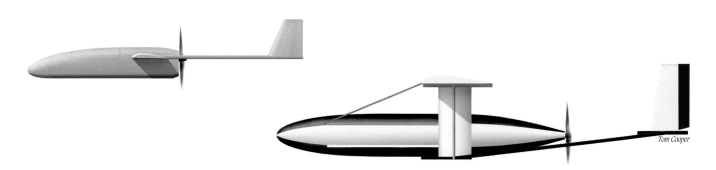

Starting in 1993, Iraq launched the development of numerous small UAVs with tactical range. Work at the Ibn Firnas Centre eventually resulted in the emergence of a wide range of models, all based on commercial components and designated Yamamah 1 through to Yamamah 11. Most were piston engine powered though some used jets. The first to enter production and operational service was Yamamah 2, developed into the Musayara-20, shown to the left. Meanwhile, a more ambitious project, launched in 2000, resulted in the development of the al-Qods UAV, shown to the right, designed for electronic warfare. Al-Qods was about to enter series production when the US-led Coalition invaded in 2003. (Artwork by Tom Cooper)

In 1999, Iraq initiated a major project of upgrading the remaining stock of V-601 missiles for the S-125/SA-3 SAM system, and for making their launchers mobile. This resulted in the replacement of booster-stages with those from old V-755 and V-759 missiles, and the development of a new, twin-rail launcher installed on the chassis of a light Iveco truck, shown on the left side. Shown to the right is the final anti-aircraft project completed before the invasion of 2003: a Project Rushdie launcher. Essentially, each of these consisted of the gun carriage from a Czechoslovak-made M53 cannon, with two tubes from a BM-21 launcher. Aiming was undertaken visually and with the help of radars: for example, in 2001, the Iraqis developed a ground-based radar from the N010 radar of a MiG-29 destroyed in an earlier Allied air strike – the emissions of which initially prompted the US and the British crews underway over Iraq into the wrong assumption that the Iraqis were operating Russian-made S-300 (ASCC/NATO codename 'SA-10 Grumble') SAM systems. (Artwork by David Bocquelet and Tom Cooper)

A photograph taken by an Iraqi MiG-25RB, showing the Iranian pontoon bridge spanning the Shatt al-Arab to connect the Abadan Peninsula with the Faw Peninsula. Made of steel pipes and Styrofoam, this bridge proved an exceptionally survivable construction. (Tom Cooper collection)

loss of several Sukhois. Eventually, the Iraqis found the solution in combining Soviet-made Kh-29Ls with French-made PD-LCT Patric laser designators: the advantage of the latter was that it was installed under the aircraft, and – once locked-on on the target – enabled the pilot to turn away from the combat zone, free to perform avoidance manoeuvres. Related testing was conducted in September 1987, and resulted in the development of tactics in which the Iraqis would first seek to suppress Iranian air defences through the usual combination of Mirages equipped with Syrel, Caiman, Remora, and Baz-AR and Su-22M-2Ks armed with Kh-28s, before Patric-equipped Mirage F.1EQ-5s marked the target for Kh-29Ls released either by Su-22M-3Ks or the latest Su-22M-4s. Following extensive preparations, this attack was flown on 17 April 1988, essentially opening the Iraqi offensive for the liberation of Faw. It included four Mirage F.1EQ-5s marking targets for an entire squadron of Su-22M-4s. The bridge was hit at at least six points, cut off from its anchor on either bank and floated down the Shatt al-Arab, falling apart in the process. The crucial lifeline of the Iranian troops on the Faw Peninsula was thus cut off right at the start of the Iraqi offensive – which ended with a quick and complete success. In May 1988, the combination of one PD-LCT-equipped Mirage and four Kh-29-equipped Su-22M-3Ks from No. 69 Squadron was deployed to strike two Styrofoam-supported pontoon bridges on the Karoun River. Facing less resistance than over the Faw, this time the Iraqis required less than two minutes and only four Kh-29Ls to score four precise hits: both bridges were cut from their anchors and thus disabled. Ultimately, the success of this combination emboldened the Technical Department of the IrAF to the point where they decided to install Kh-29Ls directly onto Mirage F.1EQ-5s and thus replace very expensive French-made AS.30L laser-guided missiles with much cheaper Soviet weapons. The work on this combination was completed only in early 1989, and it was never deployed in combat.

UNGUIDED ATOLLS

Another Iraqi modification emerged around the same time and addressed the problem of attack and assault helicopters of the IrAF and the Army Aviation Corps (IrAAC) lacking a heavy unguided rocket suitable for attacks from outside the range of 23mm light anti-aircraft guns, and MANPADs operated in large numbers by the Iranian infantry. For similar reasons, the Iraqi Army was searching for a similar weapon. The solution was found in a stock of obsolete R-3S air-to-air missiles, withdrawn from service in the early 1980s. One of the workshops at Camp Taji removed the infrared seeker head from the front of the missile, installed an M-46 130mm artillery shell instead, and fixed the steering fins by welding them in the 'straight ahead' position. The weapon was successfully tested on a Soviet-made BMP-1 infantry fighting vehicle that had its turret removed and replaced by a simple mechanism including six launch rails. After successful testing, it was pressed into service by ground forces in

A Kh-29L missile captured in Iraq in 2003. (US DoD)

early 1988, and by April was also in use on Mil Mi-8 helicopters of the IrAAC.

Following the success of the modified R-3S, the MIC inspected stocks of other older missiles, and amongst them found a number of the large R-40s (ASCC/NATO codename 'AA-6 Acrid') – used by MiG-25PD (export) interceptors – that had had more than 50 'trips' on an aircraft. The rounds in question were modified through the removal and replacement of their seeker heads by a contact fuse. Under Project Nasser, four modified missiles were installed on a MiG-25 interceptor for flight testing, and fired from an altitude of 10,000m (32,808ft) and range of 80km from the target. Much to the disappointment of the involved team, all four fell not only well away from the target but their detonations were relatively small, leaving large parts of the missiles intact. Uncertain how to regulate the range and improve the precision, the team abandoned this project. That said, in 1990 the same team was ordered to subject the remaining stocks of RS-2U air-to-air missiles (ASCC/NATO codename 'AA-1 Alkali') to a similar modification as used on the R-3S: Iraq still had about 50 of these left from its stillborn acquisition of MiG-19PM interceptors from the USSR in 1959–1960, and in 1973 it acquired 100 additional rounds from Bulgaria. As in the case of the R-3S, the conversion was relatively straightforward: the infrared seeker head was removed from the front of the missile and replaced with a 120mm mortar bomb. The entire stock of modified RS-2Us was expended by helicopter units of the IrAAC by the end of the war.

END OF WAR WITH IRAN

Despite defensive success, Saddam considered the Iranian conquest of Halabja to be a violation of the UN-negotiated agreement that ended the Second War of the Cities. Moreover, the week-long break in missile firings enabled Hussein Kamil and Saadi to arrange a massive increase in conversions of R-17Es to al-Husseins at the al-Mustafa Factory: by now, each of its three workshops had four production lines, each of which began turning out one new missile a day, for a total of 12 every 24 hours. Therefore, as soon as the situation on the frontlines stabilised, Missile Brigade 224 was in action with full force. Between 16 March and 20 April 1988, it fired no fewer than 120 al-Husseins at Arak, Tehran, Kashan, Tabriz, and Shiraz. As far as the Iraqis knew, all but two missiles – which failed to detonate due to well-known problems with their batteries – functioned as expected. Their effect was beyond expectations: estimates differ, but between one quarter and one third of the 10-million population of the Iranian capital fled outside the city. As morale in Iraq – further bolstered by a successful offensive that recovered the Faw Peninsula, in April 1988 – soared, that in Iran collapsed as the result of this blow.

Statistics for ballistic missile warfare during the Iran–Iraq War remain only partially available: while total figures for the number of FROG-7s and R-17Es launched in 1980–1982 are known, there is no breakdown by type. On the contrary, depending on the source, Iraq is known to have launched a total of 361 R-17Es and 188 or 189 al-Husseins between 1982 and 1988 (in contrast, Iran fired only 117 R-17s and Hwasong-5s: most of these – about 60 in total – targeted Baghdad). Of the al-Husseins, 135 are known to have hit Tehran, causing at least 1,150 fatalities and more than 4,000 injured.[5]

Arguably, the ballistic missiles in question caused relatively little material and physical damage: however, they delivered strong psychological and political blows. Indeed, combined with IrAF air strikes on Iranian oil refineries, the Second War of the Cities especially caused a fundamental change in the geostrategic scenario of this war. While early during the conflict it was the IRIAF that was

A pair of al-Hussein missiles on display during the arms trade show in Baghdad in May 1989. Both missiles were shown installed on 'fixed' launchers. (Photo by Peter Foster)

better equipped and capable of striking deep into Iraq, demolishing its oil industry, by 1988 it was the IrAF and the Iraqi Army's missile units that were delivering not only far more numerous, but far heavier blows upon Iran. This combination of air and missile strikes played a crucial role in forcing Tehran to accept UN Security Council Resolution 598, which called for a ceasefire between Iran and Iraq: 20 August thus became the last day of the Iran–Iraq War.

9

COMING OF AGE

In March 1988, in recognition of the success in producing the al-Hussein, the MIC was made a part of the newly created Ministry of Industry and Military Industrialisation (MIMI). Command over this body was given to Hussein Kamil (promoted to general for this purpose), who by the time was one of the most powerful men in Iraq, responsible for a wide variety of military and civilian industrial projects. The Surface-to-Surface Missile Research and Development team was incorporated into the new organisation, and Saadi appointed the First Deputy Minister of the MIMI. This was the result of the synergy of more than 15 years of massive investment into the training of the necessary workforce, the acquisition and construction of development and research facilities, the construction of the necessary industrial infrastructure, and the success of Project al-Hussein, had profound effects upon the Iraqi defence sector. The MIMI significantly accelerated the work of the Iraqi defence sector which soon bristled with ever additional projects of the kind like al-Hussein: many of these aimed to further improve available weapons through stretching their range, but at least a few aimed to create entirely new weapons systems with the help of high technology acquired from abroad.

However, amid the general optimism in Iraq of the following period, many overlooked the fact that the country's economy was exhausted and heavily indebted. Certainly enough, Saddam and the RCC remained demonstratively optimistic, promising full recovery in a matter of years. However, not only were they slow in demobilising the massive armed forces built up during eight years of war but continued lavishly spending for defence purposes although there was ever less money to do so. That said, the MIC began emphasising further development of the domestic industries above everything else. As a result, the work of Iraqi engineers and scientists continued at quite a high pace, resulting in an entire series of new projects.

SSMD

Shortly before the end of the war with Iran, all rocket and missile equipped units of the Iraqi Army and the Republican Guards Forces Command were reassigned from the Army's Artillery Directorate to a new, corps-level body, designated the Surface-to-Surface Missile Directorate (SSMD). Commanded by Lieutenant General Hazem Abd al-Razzaq al-Ayyoubi, the SSMD assumed control of all the three existing missile brigades, and – just like the SSMRD – was subordinated directly to Saddam Hussein.

PROJECT 1728

Once the first phase of conversion of al-Hussein missiles was completed, Saadi's team was reorganised into six sub-teams, codenamed as follows:

- 144/1 was the management of the project
- 144/2 was manufacturing missile bodies
- 144/3 was a group working on manufacturing equipment
- 144/4 was responsible for reverse engineering of the gyroscope and guidance system
- 144/5 was working on reverse engineering the engine
- 144/6 was responsible for manufacturing new launchers

Efforts to acquire the necessary machinery and tools began in 1988 and were primarily focused on contacting West German companies. Priority was given to the equipment necessary to process metal for fuel tanks, and the related cutting and welding. Furthermore, within Project 1728, the MIC placed an order with the Thyssen Corporation for 305 turbopumps. Arguably, this effort shared the fate of Project 235, i.e. the Condor/Badr-2000, and was stopped in 1990 for reasons described below, while only partially completed. However, by then the Iraqis had received 35 German-made turbopumps, related machinery and parts worth DM38 million – from Thysen and from a company named Iwako – together with additional know-how and assistance from enterprises in Austria, Brazil, Great Britain, and the USA. The net result was that the Iraqi missile industry became capable of independent testing of indigenously assembled engines and airframes, and of indigenous production and assembly of entire airframes and most of the parts of control and guidance systems, and complete liquid-fuelled motors.

PROJECT AL-ABBAS

In 1988, Team 144/1 successfully developed the first improvement of the al-Hussein missile. Named al-Abbas, and still based on the

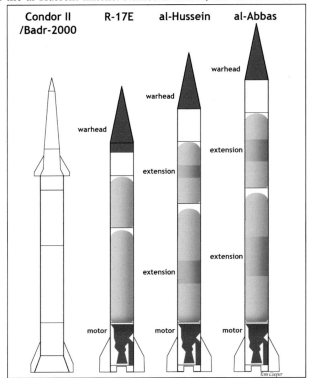

A simplified diagram comparing (from left to right) Argentine/Iraqi/Egyptian Condor II/Badr-2000, the R-17E, the al-Hussein, and the al-Abbas. Al-Hussein was the only one to actually enter operational service: it was 12.46m long, had a capacity of 4,500kg of liquid propellant (22 percent kerosene and 78 percent IRFNA), and a launch weight of 6,500kg. (Diagram by Tom Cooper)

An al-Abbas missile put on display at the May 1989 arms fair in Baghdad. It was stretched to 13.75m, had a launch weight of 7,870kg, and was intended to have an entirely new guidance and control system developed in cooperation between Iraqi, Brazilian, and West German experts. (via Ali Tobchi)

'chassis' of the R-17E, this was intended to develop a weapon with a range of 950km. For this purpose, the missile body was stretched to 13.75m. Including a warhead of only 225kg, it had a total launch weight of 7,870kg and was designed to become deployable from the same indigenous TEL as al-Hussein. Above all, the al-Abbas had an entirely new guidance system developed in Brazil. Test launches proved not only its ability to fly over 900km, but that it was much more precise than al-Hussein, having repeatedly landed within 500

An al-Wallid TEL used for the al-Hussein missile: four of the six that were completed by 1990 were assigned to the newly established Brigade 223. (Ali Tobchi collection)

metres of its target. However, in April 1987, the USA, Canada, France, West Germany, Italy, Japan, and Great Britain signed the Missile Technology Control Regime, which banned the export of most missiles and their components. Moreover, in 1990, the newly elected President George Bush started to pay more attention to the policies of Saddam Hussein. As a result, he not only effected the ultimate end of Project Condor II/Badr-2000, but also a slowdown of Brazilian involvement in Project al-Abbas. The final nail in the coffin of the latter was delivered by the UN arms embargo imposed after the Iraqi invasion of Kuwait in August 1990, resulting in al-Abbas never entering production nor operational service.

PROJECT AL-WALLID

Parallel with the work on additional missiles, Team 144/6 launched the development of an indigenous transporter-erector-launcher. This proved a relatively straightforward issue, solved with the help of reverse engineering. The primary difference was that instead of reverse engineering the entire MAZ-543 TEL, Team 144/6, led by engineer Wallid Alawi, only reverse-manufactured the launcher, and mounted it on commercial trailers, more than 70 of which were acquired for this purpose from abroad. Team 144/6 produced six trailer-mounted launchers designated al-Wallid, in 1989–1990. While two of these were kept back for testing and training purposes, the other four were used in April 1990 to equip an entirely new unit of the SSMD: Brigade 223, based in Camp Taji.

PROJECT AL-AABED

In 1989, the Salahuddin Works launched work on the development of the first Iraqi communication satellite, designated Tamouz-1. Obviously, such a project required a suitable carrier missile, and – as could be expected – this task was assigned to the team led by Lieutenant General Amer as-Saadi. This time, Saadi opted to develop a three-stage design. Starting at the bottom – i.e. the first stage – his team strapped together five motor sections from al-Hussein missiles. The second stage was based on the design for al-Hussein. However, the development of the crucial third stage, one which was to carry a payload of up to 750kg, was never completed as Iraq lacked the know-how and capability to manufacture the insulation necessary for protecting the very tip of the missile. Therefore, on the first prototype of the resulting missile, named al-Aabed, only the first stage was operational, while both the second and the third stage carried ballast weights.

Al-Aabed was a massive construction, about 23m long and weighing about 48,000kg on launch. The first – and only – test launch took place on 5 December 1989, and the first stage worked as expected. Thanks to reinforcements based on calculations provided by Gerald Bull, and modified control vanes, the cluster of

A front view of the al-Wallid TEL with an al-Hussein missile (for further details, see colour section). (Ali Tobchi collection)

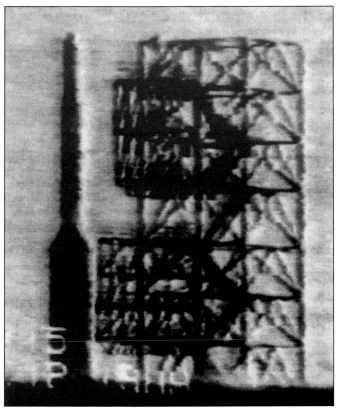

A still from a video released by Iraqi National TV, showing the outlines of the al-Aabed missile (officially described as a carrier for the Thammuz 1 satellite), prior to the test launch from the al-Anbar Space Research Centre, on 5 December 1988. (via Ali Tobchi)

five al-Hussein motor sections survived the lift-off and reached an altitude of 12,000 metres before exhausting its fuel and successfully separating from the second stage. Interestingly, not understanding the nature of this test – probably because they did not know that the second stage of the al-Aabed was still undergoing research and development – Western observers widely considered it to be a failure. Further confusion was caused by an announcement from Baghdad, later the same month, that Iraq was in the process of developing yet another new ballistic missile, including a first stage

made from the R-17E, and the second stage from an SA-2 SAM. Actually, at that point in time, the Iraqis simply lacked the materials and know-how for the development of the second stage and, due to the failure of Project 395, and then the assassination of Gerald Bull, this was to remain that way forever.

That said, parallel to Project al-Aabed, the SSMRD was working on a similar three-stage rocket for military purposes. Codenamed Project Tammuz, and developed with some help from companies in France and Germany, this was expected to result in a weapon capable of carrying a 1.25m-long warhead over a range of 1,200–1,600km. Research and development were planned to be complete by 1993, but the project was abandoned in 1990–1991.

PROJECTS LAITH & RA'AD

As Project al-Hussein reached an advanced stage, several of the involved experts became free to initiate work on a similar development of the 9M21 rocket of the Luna-9M/FROG-7 system. Thus came into being Project al-Laith: this resulted in extending the range from 70 to 100km, and the installation of a new trajectory balancer (i.e. gyroscope), which significantly increased precision. Moreover, the conventional warhead was replaced with one containing submunitions. This part of the project eventually led to the development of three slightly different missiles:

- Laith was equipped with a warhead that opened its front when it reached an altitude of 100–300 metres above the target area. The strong airstream then scattered cylindrical bomblets over the target zone, making this weapon suitable for attacks on enemy troop concentrations.
- Ra'ad was equipped with a more sophisticated 'diffuser' type of warhead, designed to be released in a 'swoop', instead of vertically. The warhead activated as the missile descended to about 400 metres above the ground and within about one second released 300 cylindrical bomblets from two sides of the rear part of the warhead. This made this version more suitable for attacks on columns of armour or other vehicles, as well as columns of infantry.
- Fateh, with a range of 150km and a warhead containing 400 bomblets, was the longest ranged of the modified Iraqi 9M21s.

The total number of 9M21s converted to these standards, as well as most details of their combat deployment during the war for Kuwait in 1991, remain unknown. What is known is that Project Laith was deployed in combat during that conflict and then continued through the 1990s. Not only were a number of operational examples put on display during a military parade in Baghdad in 2001, but they were deployed in combat against the US-led invasion of 2003, even if all were misidentified as 'Frog-7' by their opponents.

A 9M21 rocket of the Luna-98M/FROG-7 system, from Brigade 225, in firing position during one of the test firings of Project Laith in 1989. Eventually, the complete stock of this type of missile was reworked by 1991. (Ali Tobchi collection)

CONVERTED SAMS

Once the war with Iran was over, the IrAF found itself in possession of large stocks of obsolete missiles and surface-to-air missiles (SAMs) that were deemed surplus to the requirement. In 1988, the MIC and the SSMRD thus decided to use the oldest remaining examples for other purposes. Included in this selection were missiles from systems like the S-75 Volkhov, Volga, and Dvina (ASCC/NATO codename 'SA-2 Guideline'), S-125 Pechora ('SA-3 Goa'), and 2K12 Kub ('SA-6 Gainful'). Prior to starting any kind of work, the teams involved ran careful studies on the missiles in question, before trying to figure out how to improve their range to about 150 kilometres (or more), while retaining their precision and reliability. In almost all cases, the conclusion was relatively simple: they had to weld the steering fins into a fixed position, to prevent them from moving, and to remove their seeker heads and proximity fuses, while replacing theses with an additional warhead weighing 100kg, and armed with a contact fuse.

The large stock of V-755 and V-759 missiles of the S-75/SA-2 SAM system led the MIC to the idea of deploying these as ballistic missiles. The S-75 already had a surface-to-surface mode, but its fire-control radar (ASCC/NATO codename 'Fan Song') required a target with a large radar cross section in order to be precisely guided. Within the framework of Project Fahad, initiated in 1988, the Iraqis aimed to convert a stock of old V-755s and V-759s into 'pure' ballistic missiles that would require no radar guidance at all. Colonel Ahmad Sadik Rushdie al-Astrabadi – an officer of the IrAF Intelligence Directorate with rich experience in cooperation with the French and the MIC – was reassigned to the SSMRD to act as the director of this program. His team eventually developed two variants: one with a range of 300km and the other with a range of 500km. Between the summer of 1988 and early 1990, 21 test launches were undertaken, but the work on the shorter-ranged version was abandoned during the research and development stage. The 500km version was put on display at the 1989 Baghdad Arms Exhibition, under the designation Fahad, but cancelled in July of the same year. Nevertheless, the related work was relaunched in the 1990s, when it formed the basis for several new missiles.

The second series of SAMs modified to ballistic missiles, that reached the stage of flight testing, were V-601s of the S-125/SA-3 system. A number of modified rounds were brought to the Husyba area in southern Iraq for testing purposes. However, when the missile was fired, it flew so far off course that it crashed in the empty semi-desert of eastern Syria. After throughout checks, the second test launch was undertaken from the same site, and the missile hit the ground about 250 kilometres away. Although the team of engineers involved was satisfied, and one such modified SA-3 was put on display during the May 1989 arms fair in Baghdad under the codename Barq, the project was cancelled at that point in time.

Meanwhile, the same team attempted the same with 3M9 missiles of the SA-6 system: a number of rounds – all older than seven years, and meanwhile sent to the USSR for overhaul – was selected for a possible modification. However, while studying them, the Iraqis concluded that 'locking' their fins in a fixed position was likely to become as hard as replacing the seeker head with an additional warhead and contact fuse. Thus, although additional studies were carried out for a while longer and one of the prototypes was put on display in Baghdad in May 1989, under the designation Kaser, the project was cancelled following Iraq's invasion of Kuwait on 2 August 1990.

PROJECT AL-FAW

Between 1971 and 1988, Iraq imported a total of 46 S-75 SAM systems and at least 2,016 associated V-755 and V-759 missiles. Over the same period, only about 100 of these were fired for testing and training purposes or spent in combat. Thus, as of 1988, the IrAF was still in possession of a sizeable stock. The successful deployment of the al-Hussein missile against Iran not only emboldened but concerned the High Command in Baghdad: after all it was perfectly possible that they might encounter an enemy equipped with ballistic missiles, whether Iran or Israel. Therefore, in late spring 1988, the High Command in Baghdad requested that the MIC find a solution for anti-ballistic missile defence. The MIC organised a team led by Lieutenant General Amer al-Ubaidy. Knowing there was no way to import suitable weapons systems from abroad, Ubaidy decided to make use of the effectively surplus stock of old SA-2s. The radars and fire-control systems proved capable of detecting and tracking incoming ballistic missiles, but the missiles turned out to need a much more advanced fuse, to enable their timely detonation in the light of the immense speeds at which the two weapons would approach each other. This task was assigned to Amer al-Awaidy's team, which was working at Camp Taji. As the necessary modified fuses became available, Ubaidy's team initiated a series of test firings, all carried out at a site about 200km south of Baghdad. They pushed very hard, eventually spending 63 modified V-755s and V-759s, and 16 Lunas before obtaining acceptable results, including a number of direct hits. The project was declared a success and the modified missiles were officially accepted into service under the designation al-Faw. All the available examples were distributed to the SA-2 SAM sites of the IrAF by 1990. The only problem was that the system never encountered a suitable target: during the war of 1991, the Americans deployed cruise missiles, but no ballistic missiles. Thus, although successful, the al-Faw was never deployed in combat.

A V-755 or V-759 missile of the S-75/SA-2 SAM system modified as a ballistic missile, seen after its capture in 2003. (Tom Cooper collection)

Table 1: Iraqi Missile Industry, 1988–1991[1]

Project/Facility	Product	Site
Project 144.2 Mustafa	production of R-17/al-Hussein missiles	Camp Taji
Project 1728/Project 144.3 Mutawakeel	production of engines for al-Hussein	Camp Taji, Rafah, Khadmiya, Shahiyat
Project 144.4 Karama	production of guidance systems for al-Hussein	Wazeriya
Project 144.5 Farooq	production of launchers for al-Hussein	Qa'aqa, Dora
Project 144.7	production of liquid propellant for al-Hussein	Qa'aqa
Khalid Factory	production of warheads for al-Hussein	Qa'aqa
Badr-2000	production and testing of Badr-2000	Yawn al-Azim/Belat ash-Shuhada
Badr-2000	production of motor cases for Badr-2000	Thu al-Fiqar/Belat ash-Shuhada
Badr-2000	production of solid propellant for Badr-2000	Taj al-Marik/Belat ash-Shuhada
Nasser State Establishment	production of al-Hussein and Badr-2000 missiles, involvement in Supergun program	
Badr State Establishment	production of al-Hussein and Badr-2000 missiles	
Qadessiya State Establishment	production of al-Hussein missiles	
Saddam State Establishment	Production of al-Hussein missiles, involvement in Supergun program	
Qa'aqa State Establishment	production of components for al-Hussein missiles, involvement in Supergun program	
State Establishment for Automobile Industries	production of components for al-Hussein missiles	
State Establishment for Mechanical Industries	production of components for al-Hussein missiles	
Salahuddin State Establishment	production of components for al-Hussein missiles	
Kindi State Establishment	production of components for al-Hussein missiles, involvement in Supergun program	
Nida Factory	production of components for al-Hussein missiles	
Harith Factory	production of indigenously developed missile engines	
Numan Factory	production of indigenously developed missile engines	

PROJECT FAW-150

The success of Project 144 led to the idea of attempting to stretch the range of several other, older Soviet weapons systems in their arsenals. Amongst these was the P-15 Termit anti-ship missile (ASCC/NATO codename 'SS-N-2 Styx'), famous from the Egyptian sinking of the Israeli destroyer *Eilat* in 1967. Work on stretching the range of the Styx followed the same principles as the work on al-Hussein: the missile body – originally 6.55m long – was cut in two, and an additional section was inserted, including a bigger liquid-propellant tank. The resulting weapon was designated Faw, was about 8.9m long, and had a range increased from 70 to 150km. All the other components – including an autopilot for the mid-course guidance, and the terminal phase active radar seeker – were retained as they were. The work on the Faw-150 was completed in 1990, and the missile entered operational service during the same year. The conversion process included the use of numerous Chinese-made HY-1 and HY-2 missiles, based on the P-15 design. Project Faw-200 was initiated as soon as the Faw-150 was accepted for operational service in 1990. However, related facilities were bombed out during the war of 1991, and thus this project had to be cancelled.

PROJECT BAGHDAD

During the eight-year war with Iran, the IrAF was constantly troubled by the poor low-altitude radar coverage. With the Saad-13 factory already manufacturing local versions of the TRS-2105 Tigre-G early warning radars under the designation SDA-G, and with the IrAF eventually acquiring more than 40 Ilyushin Il-76MD transports, the idea was born to develop an airborne early warning and control system (AWACS). The resulting Project Baghdad was initiated in 1988, with the aim of matching the existing radar and airframe.

The first solution developed by the Salahuddin Works was to install a single SDA-G antenna within the loading ramp, in an upside-down position, and cover it with a plastic radome. The support equipment, including four consoles for operators, was installed within the cargo cabin. Obviously, this was far from ideal, as the radar was thus able to scan only a 180-degree wide arc to the rear of the aircraft. Moreover, the selected radar caused manifold problems. The Tigre-G was optimised for support of short-ranged anti-aircraft defences, and capable of detecting low-flying aircraft out to a range of 100km (62nm) and proved useful for coastal surveillance and support of shore-based anti-shipping missiles. Indeed, the SDA-G installed in the first Il-76 selected for conversion (a jet usually assigned to No. 43 Squadron, IrAF) proved to have a range of no less than 350 kilometres. However, it also proved susceptible to ground clutter. Moreover, some foreigners who had an opportunity to examine the Baghdad-1 quickly concluded that if used for any

A top view of the Chinese-manufactured version of the P-15 Termit, best-known in Iraq as HY-1/2. (via Ali Tobchi)

length of time, its installation would probably microwave its own crew for the lack of screening inside the fuselage.

Unsurprisingly, the Baghdad was effectively abandoned before its first flight test, and the Technical Department of the IrAF refocused its attention on a more conventional model, including an oval-shaped rotating radome made of fibreglass, with diameter of 9 metres, mounted atop a pedestal above the fuselage. Tragically, the prototype of this project crashed – due to a design error – during its first flight, killing the crew and numerous engineers, and the Iraqis found themselves with no choice but to request help from France.

Initiated in 1989, the third Iraqi attempt to make an AWACS aircraft was conducted as Project Adnan – after the late Minister of Defence, Adnan Khairallah, killed in a crash in that year. It was subjected to the direct control of Amer Rashid and was run by the Salahuddin Works but in cooperation with several French companies. Like the Baghdad before, the Adnan received the SDA-G radar (redesignated the Salahuddin-G for this purpose). Other mission equipment was of Italian (Selenia) and British (Marconi) origin, while the Identification Friend or Foe system was made by Collins (nowadays Collins Aerospace, a unit of Raytheon Technologies Corporation). The Adnan promptly proved highly promising: during flight testing, the radar regularly detected and tracked aircraft with a radar cross section of two square metres from

The rear fuselage and fin of the sole Baghdad-1, with the plastic dome covering the installation of the Tigre-G radar in the rear of the cargo bay. Notably the aircraft still wore the livery of Iraqi Airways, although always operated by No. 33 Squadron, IrAF. (Photo by Peter Foster)

One of more than 40 Iraqi Ilyushin Il-76MD transports. All were operated by Nos. 33 and 43 Squadrons, IrAF, but always wore civilian livery. Indeed, in support of the transfer of Mirages from France via Greece and Turkey to Iraq, several temporarily wore the livery of a Jordanian airline. (Tom Cooper collection)

Probably the best photograph of an Adnan AWACS. Of interest is one of the strakes installed on the rear fuselage: the Iraqis installed them in a significantly higher position than that of similar strakes on the genuine Soviet/Russian A-50 AWACS. (Tom Cooper collection)

The sole Adnan-1 seen passing over Baghdad during a parade in 1989, together with two MiG-29s, one of which is visible here. (Ali Tobchi collection)

to its invasion of Kuwait. The sole Adnan-1 prototype was destroyed on that night by US laser-guided bombs used against Taqaddum AB. The Baghdad-1 and Adnan-2 were then evacuated to Iran following an order from the government: Iran confiscated and – although failing to make them operational again – never returned them to Iraq.[2]

ONE-OFFS

Much less is known about several 'minor' projects conducted by or on behalf of the Iraqi Air Force during the second half of 1980s, both of which were originally related to reconnaissance tasks. The first of these was initiated in 1986, when the Director of the IrAF Intelligence Department, Brigadier General Mudher al-Farhan, was seeking a way to obtain reconnaissance photographs of several oil loading terminals constructed by the Iranians in the lower Persian Gulf. The GMID offered him one of its Dassault Falcon 50s: on 24 June 1986, this aircraft flew from Amman in Jordan, via Kuwait and down the commercial corridor along the Saudi coast, via the United Arab Emirates to India. Underway, it made an 'unintended navigational error' and passed close to the Iranian island of Sirri, enabling a photographer that was on board to take photographs. As a result, on 12 August 1986, the tanker terminal off Siri was bombed by Mirage F.1s.

The excellent range of the Falcon 50 then gave birth to the idea of equipping it with French-made AM.39 Exocet missiles. Arguably, this was nothing new, for the French had been operating several slightly smaller Dassault Falcon 20s equipped with the cockpit of their Dassault Super Etendard fighter-bomber for training purposes for a while. That said, the modification in question was beyond the IrAF's capabilities and thus Baghdad requested that Paris organise the work in question. In late 1986, a Falcon 50, registration YI-ALE, was sent to Villarohe, where it received not only a Cyrano IVQ-C5 radar in a stretched nose, but the full cockpit of the Mirage F.1EQ-5 on the right side of its cockpit, and a launcher for an AM.39 Exocet missile under each wing. Following extensive testing in France, the jet was commissioned into IrAF service in February 1987, under the official designation Yarmouk. Within the General Headquarters in Baghdad, it became known as Suzanna.

After additional testing and training in Iraq, on 17 May 1987 Suzanna flew its one and only – and most famous – combat sortie. After taking off from Wahda AB, it proceeded via Kuwait down the Saudi coast to a position north of Bahrain, where the crew turned east. After acquiring a suitable target, it released both Exocets. A few minutes later, these struck the US Navy guided-missile frigate USS *Stark* (FFG-31), killing 37 sailors. The mistake shook Baghdad, which quickly apologised for this unintentional attack and compensated the Pentagon and the families for the sailors killed and for all the damage caused. This was not the end of Suzanna though. By 1989, the aircraft had undergone additional modification and it received an additional fuel tank installed in the cabin, and a hardpoint under the fuselage enabling it to load yet more fuel in the RP.35 drop tank usually carried by Mirages. Atop of that, it was equipped with installations necessary to carry a Raphael TH

a range of 350 kilometres (217 miles), with 80 percent accuracy regarding the range and exact position. Amer Rashid thus promptly ordered the conversion of a second Il-76 to the same standard, the radar of which was expected to have the range of 450 kilometres (280 miles). The aircraft selected for this project was an Il-76MD with construction number 0033449455. The total 'production run' thus included one Baghdad-1 and one Adnan-1 (0033449455 and 0083484542 respectively), and one Adnan-1 upgraded to the Adnan-2 standard, the development of which was never completed.

As of 1990–1991, all four aircraft (the sole Baghdad-1 was still used for testing various subassemblies) were still undergoing flight testing prior to their acceptance to operational service with the IrAF. Correspondingly, none was airborne during the night of 15 to 16 January 1991 when the US-led Coalition attacked Iraq as a response

A group photo of the top engineers of the Projects Baghdad/Adnan-1/Adnan-2, in front of the sole Adnan-1, and in company of General Amer Rashid (fifth from left). Clearly visible in the rear is the radome containing a heavily modified antenna of the Tigre-G radar. (Ali Tobchi collection)

A rare still from a video showing the only Adnan-2 taxiing for take-off, as released by the Iraqi News Agency in August 1990. The aircraft was easily recognisable by its camouflage pattern in two shades of grey. While highly promising, it never entered operational service with the IrAF and was destroyed on the ground during the first night of the 1991 war. (Tom Cooper collection)

A still from a video showing the 'Suzanna' after her modifications of 1988–1989. In addition to the radome of the Mirage F.1EQ-5 attached to the nose, visible under the aircraft is a Raphael TH reconnaissance pod. (Tom Cooper collection)

reconnaissance pod: this included a side-looking radar (SLAR) and a datalink that enabled the transfer of collected intelligence to a ground base in real time. At least in theory, Suzanna thus became one of the most powerful clandestine intelligence assets in the Middle East. Moreover, it possessed the capability to – equipped with two AM.39s – reach the 'Eastern Mediterranean area' and carry out anti-ship and reconnaissance operations there. Alas, the IrAF was not happy with the Raphael TH though, and with the French never finding time to sort out the related problems, the jet saw no further action. In February 1991, it was 'evacuated' to Iran, together with more than 130 other aircraft of the IrAF and Iraqi Airways.[3]

That said, the experience with Suzanna meanwhile led the IrAF to another idea. The result was the least well known of all the Iraqi projects related to an aircraft, possibly codenamed Faw-727. Essentially, this was a Boeing 727 airliner of Iraqi Airways, taken over by the IrAF, and then heavily modified – probably at the Salahuddin Works, possibly with some French support. There are several entirely different versions about the nature of the modifications in question: one is that Faw-727 was equipped as an airborne command post; another that it was equipped with the TMV-018 Syrel electronic intelligence gathering system (usually installed in the form of a pod carried under the centreline of Mirage F.1EQ-2s), and an improved sub-variant of the Raphael TH pod; the third was that it was equipped with electronic warfare systems like the TMV-002 Remora and TMV-004 Caiman and acted as an airborne stand-off jammer. Sadly, precise details have never became available: the only detail known about Faw-727 is that it was airborne during the Iraqi invasion of Kuwait on 2 August 1990.

Another Iraqi project of the late 1980s using a combination of French and Soviet military technology, was the installation of French-made IFR probes on a handful of MiG-23BN and Su-22M-4 fighter-bombers of the IrAF. Flight testing – as in this case, showing a Sukhoi receiving fuel from a Douglas D704 pod carried by a Mirage F.1EQ-4 – validated the idea. However, Iraq ran out of time to acquire enough probes for their fleet-wide application, and the necessary training of crews. (Ali Tobchi collection)

10
THE LEGACIES OF SAADI AND BULL

Late in 1987, the Iraqi government re-established contact with Gerald Bull – who now worked at the SRC's Brussels office most of the time – and invited him to visit Baghdad. Arriving there in January 1988, the Canadian – accompanied by his two sons, both of whom worked for his company – met the head of the MIMI, Kamil, and his Deputy, Saadi. Understanding that the SRC could not become involved in helping Iraq develop arms while the country was still embroiled in the war with Iran, the Iraqis proposed two projects: one, official, was for Bull to provide engineering advice in regards of Iraq's space programme and domestic manufacturing facilities for the training of additional workers. The other, unofficial offer – made by Saadi to Bull only – was for the Canadian to help in the development of the al-Aabed missile, described in a previous chapter, the purpose of which, at least nominally, was of purely civilian nature. At that point, Bull informed Saadi about his decades-old passion: the idea of constructing a gun capable of launching commercial satellites into orbit – as a complement to the al-Aabed. The Iraqi was keen to hear more: following further negotiations in Brussels in early March 1988, the Canadian was requested to prepare a formal project proposal. The latter was approved by the MIMI, which agreed to finance Bull's 'supergun' with a total of US$25 million.

PROJECT BABYLON

Intending to put a payload of 2,000kg into orbit – the minimum for a contemporary commercial satellite – while understanding that he still had to conduct much research and development for this to work, Bull and the staff at the SRC developed designs for two guns.[1]

Babylon, the main gun, was to have a smoothbore barrel of 1,000mm calibre, consisting of 26 sections bolted together to a staggering length of 156 metres, weighing about 1,665 tons. Other major pieces of its equipment included four recoil cylinders (weighing 60 tons each), two buffer cylinders (weighing 7 tons each), and a 182-ton breech. Around the breech – made of steel with a tensile strength of more than 1,250 Mega Pascals – the barrel was to be 30cm thick to withstand a maximum operating pressure of 70,000psi. The overall weight of the gun was thus to grow to around 2,100 tons. Baby Babylon was to serve as a prototype and was thus much smaller. It had a 46-metre long barrel with a 350mm bore, weighed about 113 tons, and was to be of self-recoiling construction and thus mounted on rails.

Both guns were to be mounted horizontally, and – due to their sheer size and weight – could neither be moved, nor aimed. More was not necessary, however, because their purpose was of purely civilian nature: indeed, they made no sense as weapons. The detonation upon firing of Babylon was certain to create a fireball of about 90 metres diameter, and the power sufficient to be registered by seismographs

Table 2: Iraqi Superguns and their Parts[2]		
Expenditure	Declared Quantity	Fate
complete 350mm gun system	1	undergoing testing since May 1989; destroyed by UNSCOM, 1991
tubes for 350mm gun	6	destroyed by UNSCOM, 1991
steel breech for 350mm gun	1	destroyed by UNSCOM, 1991
bearings for 350mm gun	1	destroyed by UNSCOM, 1991
slugs for 350mm gun	7	unilaterally destroyed by Iraq, 1991
tubes for 1,000mm gun	44	destroyed by UNSCOM, 1991
slide bearings	15	destroyed by UNSCOM, 1991
hydraulic recoil cylinders (for 1,000mm gun)	4	destroyed by UNSCOM, 1991
brackets for 1,000mm gun	4	destroyed by UNSCOM, 1991
propellant charges for both guns	12 tones	destroyed by UNSCOM, 1991

Parts of the 1,000mm calibre Babylon Gun, found – still wrapped into their transportation packaging – at the Iskandariyah Vehicle Plant in August 1991. (Photo by H. Arvidson)

A view inside a section of the Project Babylon gun found at the same site. Neither meant nor designed to be used as a weapon, the Babylon program promised to offer a highly attractive alternative to conventional, rocket-powered satellite deployment. Like most of Bull's similar projects, beyond the sensationalism of the mainstream media, it attracted a strong reaction, bordering on disgust, from the related industry in the West. (Photo by H Arvidson)

even in the USA: Bull was certain that every military force in the world would know its exact coordinates within minutes of the gun being fired. Moreover, made of sections, the barrel would have been easy to knock out of alignment even by warheads that would miss by 1,000 metres. The only reason he preferred to keep the project secret was the fear that the USA, Israel, and Great Britain would do everything in their powers to stop its development because they did not want Iraq to have reconnaissance satellites.

The construction of two guns of such huge size was by no means easy: to a certain degree, it was reminiscent of assembling a giant puzzle, because it required the involvement of several highly specialised companies around the world. For example, the 52 barrel-sections were ordered from the British company Sheffield Forgemasters, its subsidiaries Forgemasters Engineering and River Don Castings, and the Walter Somers Company, in July 1988. All the parts were paid for by the Iraqis with an irrevocable letter of credit as soon as ready, and then shipped to Iraq.

Baby Babylon was originally assembled in a horizontal position at Jebel Sinjar (Mount Shingal). Following several initial experiments, by April 1989 it was relocated to Jebel Hamryn, near the village of Bir Ugla and thus in proximity of the Saad-16 complex, north-west of Mosul. Once there, the gun was regularly fired over the following month, using propellant derived from a solid nitroglycerine base and made by PRB in Brussels (which shipped it to Iraq via Jordan under the guise of ordinary artillery propellent): it managed to fire test slugs at speeds of about 3,000 metres per second. That said, by this time Bull was lagging with the development of the actual projectiles he intended to use to put a satellite into orbit: he did design a larger version of the Martlet IV, expected to reach a height of 27,000 metres, where the first stage rocket would ignite, and take the projectile to 48,000 metres, where the second stage would kick-in. The third and final stage was to activate at an altitude of 80,000 metres, and take the satellite to about 105,000 metres, by when it would move at a speed high enough to eventually reach orbit at an altitude between 1,700 and 2,000 kilometres. However, contrary to his usual fast work, this part of the project never reached the stage of actually being constructed. The reason was that Bull had meanwhile become involved in several other projects in Iraq, none of which was peaceful in its nature.

PROJECTS MAJNOON AND AL-FAW

By the time the first shipment of parts for Project Babylon had reached Iraq in August 1988, the war with Iran was over, and the SRC was thus free to cooperate with Iraq in the development of new weapons. Therefore, the MIMI rushed to contract Bull for self-propelled artillery pieces. Their idea was for the Canadian to design and develop two vehicles reminiscent of the G-6 Rhino, now introduced to service in South Africa: one, designated the Majnoon by the Iraqis, was to include Bull's original 155mm gun with 45 calibre-long barrel; the other, designated al-Faw, was to include a 210mm gun, and fire 109.4kg shells over a maximum range of 57km. Each of the two vehicles was to be capable of a maximum road speed of 90km/h, and a cross-country speed of 60–70km/h.

Indicating they were in hurry, but also trusting the SRC's ability to deliver, the Iraqis demanded prototypes of each to be ready by May 1989, when they planned a big military fair in Baghdad. Therefore, the SRC worked at great speed and contracted numerous French, German, and Spanish companies to manufacture parts for the guns: these were delivered to Bilbao, in Spain, for assembly by a company named Forex. Both gun prototypes were ready by late March 1989 and then flown to Baghdad by a chartered Soviet Antonov An-124 transport. Once in Iraq, the guns were installed on a chassis design bought from Czechoslovakia (modified to South African specifications and consisting of two parts that ensured the survival

The 'prototype' of the Majnoon gun, on display during the May 1989 arms fair in Baghdad. Although far from being complete, its general appearance was closely reminiscent of the South African G-6. (via Ali Tobchi)

that it was, to all intents and purposes, an empty shell.

That said, there is little doubt that both the Majnoon and al-Faw were viable projects, which could have been realised in Iraq if the Iraqis were allowed enough time. By early 1990, they had imported all the equipment, know-how, and machinery necessary for their production, partially from Western Europe, but mainly from South Africa. This included the capability to manufacture ERFB and base-bleed ammunition, and an automatic reloader which was to provide the two howitzers with a rate of fire of four shells per minute. However, the subsequent chain of events prevented the realisation of either project.

FATEFUL TAMMUZ

The events in question began in summer 1988 when Saadi not only introduced Bull to the secrets of Projects Saad-

of the crew and the gun if hit by a mine). Therefore, Saddam, Amer Rashid, and Saadi were capable of proudly presenting them at the Baghdad International Arms Fair, in May of the same year – exactly as planned. The prototype of the al-Faw, in particular, attracted lots of attention, even though nobody was let close enough to recognise

16, Badr-2000, and al-Aabed, but also of the super-secret Project Tammuz. Unwittingly, the Canadian thus fell for Hussein Kamil's and Saadi's plot in which work on the projects like Babylon, Majnoon, and al-Faw were mere bonuses: actually, the MIMI and the SSMRD wanted him to help develop nose cones capable of surviving temperatures of several thousand degrees Centigrade – as upon missile re-entry into the atmosphere – for the Tammuz missile. Possessing extensive experience in this discipline from his earlier work, Bull not only gave a series of seminars for Iraqi scientists on nose cone design and third stage separations of the satellite-launching missiles, but helped the MIMI acquire Matrix Churchill, a British manufacturer of high-technology lathes. Over the following 10 months, Matrix supplied computer-controlled lathes to Baghdad worth US$19 million and accepted a contract to establish a die-forging plant in al-Hillah, thus enabling the Iraqis to launch production of 155mm shells designed by Bull. Finally, Bull had – unsuccessfully – attempted

A view of the Baby Babylon in the position when found by UNSCOM inspectors in August 1991. It was subjected to regular testing from 1989 until Bull's death, but fired only metal slugs: satellite-carrying projectiles never left any of Bull's notebooks. (UNSCOM Photo)

to acquire the Lear Fan factory in Newtownabbey, near Belfast, equipped with state-of-the-art machinery for the production of advanced composites and carbon-fibre components for the aeronautical industry. Ironically, the Canadian considered himself to be safe, as he was regularly briefing Israeli representatives, and MI6 about his work in Iraq. Correspondingly, not only his own security, but the security measures of the entire SRC were non-existent. However, it is almost certain that precisely this aspect of Bull's work – his involvement in Iraqi missile projects that potentially threatened all of the country's neighbourhood – was what sealed his fate. On 22 March 1990, Gerald Bull was assassinated by unknown persons shortly before entering his flat in Brussels.

CATASTROPHE IN THE QAQAA COMPLEX

The other biggest single setback that the Iraqi defence sector experienced during 1988–1990 occurred on 19 August 1989, in the Qaqaa Complex, when a barrel full of TNT caught fire while positioned in a depot not designated for the storage of explosive materials. As the fire spread, many of thousands of workers employed there stopped to gaze at the rising column of smoke. The fire brigade reacted quickly and attempted dousing the flames – but the fire kept on burning. When a second barrel filled with TNT ignited, it caused a major conflagration, the force of which was described by most of survivors as being like the detonation of a nuclear bomb. The fireball was as bright as the Sun, burning dozens of onlookers with searing heat. A second detonation then occurred, resulting in a crater about 600 metres wide, and leaving thousands of survivors within a circle of several kilometres dazed by the shockwave. Those still able to walk spent the day searching for medical aid or helping excavate people from under the rubble of collapsed buildings, and evacuating them. The local hospitals were quickly overwhelmed by thousands of wounded. Exactly how many were killed remains unknown, primarily because not only the employees, but also the family members of the deceased were afraid of talking: everybody knew that Qaqaa was a sensitive security matter. Baghdad first denied this accident, but eventually admitted 30 fatalities: due to the secrecy surrounding the complex, the true number of casualties and the extent of damage never became known.

The catastrophe in the Qaqaa Complex had another negative repercussion for Iraq, too. Farzad Bazoft, a British journalist of Iranian origin conducted an investigation into this affair. He was arrested at Baghdad International Airport, in September 1989, while carrying with him 34 photographs of the al-Hila and Qaqaa complexes. After six weeks in Abu Ghraib prison, Bazoft was put in front of cameras and made to confess to being an Israeli agent. Following a one-day trial behind closed doors, he was convicted and sentenced to death on 10 March 1990, and executed five days later. In protest over his execution, Great Britain recalled its ambassador to Iraq, cancelled all ministerial visits, and ordered a stop of all the works and shipments of parts for Project Babylon to Iraq. Moreover, during the following days, not only the British, but several other Western intelligence services launched operations to seize components of not only the supergun, but all other weapons-related projects bound for Iraq, throughout Europe. This included the breach-block for the Babylon Gun, forged in Italy, and recoil mechanisms made in Germany and Switzerland. In shock, the SRC quickly withdrew from Project Babylon: left without the mastermind and all of his expertise, the Iraqis proved unable to complete its development. For similar reasons, other Western actions sealed the fate of numerous Iraqi arms programs.

AL-HUSSEIN MOD

From the Iraqi point of view, Bull's assassination, the Bazoft affair, and the wholesale clampdown on production and shipments of thousands of components for the Iraqi arms industry all had only one culprit: Israel's Mossad intelligence service. On 1 April 1990, in one of several speeches he gave during that period of time focusing on Israel, Saddam Hussein threatened to burn Israel with weapons of mass destruction if it attacked Iraq. At the time, the conventional wisdom was that this was another attempt by the strongman in Baghdad to claim regional leadership or rally the 'Arab street' to his side – because that was the tried and traditional tactic of many Middle Eastern politicians before him. Later on, others concluded that Saddam was concerned about the possible Israeli reaction to the invasion of Kuwait and thus wanted to test the Israeli reaction. For all practical purposes, the two options were not mutually exclusive: Saddam made many massive mistakes in regards of his foreign policy, but he was calculated, and pursuing his own strategy for his own reasons. Foremost, he took nothing for granted. Thus, even though eventually receiving – via the USA – something like an assurance from Tel Aviv that Israel would not attack Iraq as long as Saddam 'controlled himself', in April 1990 the strongman in Baghdad issued orders for an intensification of the work on derivatives of the al-Hussein missile. [3]

By that time, the three workshops of the al-Mustafa factory completed the conversion of the remaining R-17Es to al-Hussein standard. Saddam's order prompted them to develop what became known as the al-Hussein Mod: a version whose warhead would separate during the terminal flight phase, about 20,000 metres (65,616ft) above the target. This was important not only because it promised to improve accuracy, but because the Iraqis considered the warhead much too small to be detected and tracked by fire-control radars of contemporary anti-ballistic missile systems: thus, they expected these to be attracted to the body of the missile. In other words: Project al-Hussein Mod was to result in the development of a highly efficient missile decoy.

Thanks to Project 1728, by April 1990, the al-Mustafa factory and the teams of Project 144 became capable of designing, developing and manufacturing almost all the necessary parts. Therefore, Saddam ordered them to produce 300 new missiles, Team 144/6 to develop fixed launchers which were to be constructed in the western desert of Iraq, facing Israel, and a team of the Military Engineering Repair Factory to manufacture 10 decoys for such fixed launchers and 10 decoys for 9P119/MAZ-543 TELs.

After reviewing all the equipment, machinery, and parts that were available, Team 144 first decided to rework 70 R-17E missiles chopped to pieces during the initial work on Project al-Hussein (which was also a good opportunity to improve the skills of Team 144/3 in construction of fuel tanks). The powerplants for the first few rounds were obtained in similar fashion: Team 144/5, led by Colonel Muthir Sadiq Saba Khamis at-Tamimi, used engines spent during earlier testing (no engine could be used twice), and – with the help of Chinese companies – completely rebuilt them using, amongst others, turbopumps obtained under Project 1728. Control and guidance systems included newly built gyroscopes made with the help of German companies, Iraqi-manufactured warheads, and other locally produced items. Project al-Hussein Mod ran from 2 August 1990 until 17 January 1991: it resulted in the rebuilding and production of a total of 121 missiles. The first of these became available in time for the SSMD to carry out four test-firings with them, all of which were concluded successfully.

PROJECT AL-HIJARA

As a biproduct of Project al-Hussein Mod, Saadi's Team 144/1 drew on the idea of a warhead filled with concrete, and – together with Team 144/2 – developed the design for such a warhead to be manufactured in series. Eventually, five or six of such missiles were manufactured and named al-Hijara. One was tested in 1990, when it reached a range of 466km. Others were all spent in combat during the war of 1991.

11
THE WAR OF 1991

Saddam was concerned about a possible Israeli strike well before April 1990. Through 1989, he held several conferences with commanders of the SSM and the SSMRD in order to find out how Iraq's missile force should be developed: through the construction of fixed launchers, or additional mobile launching vehicles. Eventually, the strongman in Baghdad demanded both – and the GMID and IrAF to obtain the intelligence necessary to target Israel should the need arise. Thus began a chain of fateful events, the effects of which are felt in Iraq to this very day.

THE MANOEUVRES OF 1989–1990[1]

In mid-1989, two Mirage F.1EQ-5s from the Reconnaissance Flight of No. 79 Squadron were deployed to Jordan. Wearing the insignia of the Royal Jordanian Air Force, they were equipped with French-made Harold reconnaissance pods, capable of taking high-resolution images of objects 50 kilometres away. The Mirages flew a series of reconnaissance sorties along the armistice lines with Israel, collecting enough intelligence for the GMID to prepare a list of 32 targets, and the same number of target folders. Originally, these were distributed between the SSMD and the IrAF. On the basis of earlier experiences, the Iraqis concluded that the Israelis might attempt to carry out a similar operation to their air strike of 1981 against Osirak, though on a much larger scale, and that their primary targets would be Iraq's facilities for the production of chemical weapons, ballistic missile sites, and the dams that fed irrigation systems. Together

with Saddam's predilection to conserve the IrAF, this resulted in the SSMD becoming the primary means of striking Israel.

In September 1989, the Electrical-Mechanical Engineering Directorate of the Iraqi Armed Forces began the construction work on five operational launching sites in the western desert of Iraq and a similar number of dummies. By January 1991, a total of 28 fixed launchers, grouped into five clusters, had been constructed. On 31 January 1990, Brigade 223 ran a wargame in the course of which it simulated a response to a major Israeli air strike and fired four al-Husseins against targets in the desert south of Nasiriyah. On 18 April, the unit test-fired a missile equipped with a chemical warhead, and additional tests were undertaken later through the year, to check improvements in the propulsion and guidance systems of the al-Hussain Mod. On 19 June 1990, as part of the earliest preparations for an invasion of Kuwait, Brigade 225 was ordered to forward deploy its TELs to the Basra area. On 1 August 1990, Ayyubi then received the order to send Brigades 223 and 224 to the deserts of western Iraq, for the case of an Israeli reaction to the

Table 3: SSMD, Order of Battle, 1988–1991

Unit	Equipment	Notes
Missile Brigade 223	al-Hussein	est. 1990; equipped with 4 al-Wallid TELs
Missile Brigade 224	al-Hussein	est. 1974; including 2 battalions with 10 MAZ-543/P119 TELs
Missile Brigade 225	Luna-M	est. 1975
Missile Brigade 226	SS-30 & Ababil-50	est. 1989

Table 4: Iraqi R-17E & al-Hussein Launchers, July-August, 1977–1991[2]

Launchers	Declared Quantity	Notes
MAZ-543	10	5 destroyed by UNSCOM, 1991; 5 destroyed unilaterally by Iraq
Imported training mobile launcher	1	destroyed by UNSCOM, 1991
operational al-Nida launchers	4	destroyed unilaterally by Iraq, 1991
non-operational al-Nida launchers	2	destroyed by UNSCOM, 1991
indigenous prototype launchers	3	destroyed by UNSCOM, 1991
fixed launchers	56	destroyed by UNSCOM, 1991
completed control panels for fixed launchers	24	2 destroyed by UNSCOM, 1991, 22 destroyed unilaterally by Iraq, 1991

Table 5: Iraqi Warheads for R-17E & al-Hussein Missiles, 1977-1991[3]

Warheads	Declared Quantity	Source
pre-1980 expenditure	8	
Iran–Iraq War, 1980–1981	515	Iraqi documentation
testing, 1985–1990	52 imported, 12 indigenous	Iraqi documentation
Gulf War, 1991	87 imported, 6 indigenous	Iraqi documentation & independent sources
destroyed under SCR 687, July 1991	37 imported, 13 indigenous	UNSCOM verification; out of 37 imported, 15 warheads were 'conventional' and 22 'special'; out of 13 indigenous warheads, 5 were 'conventional' and 8 'special'
unilateral destruction, July–October 1991	120 imported, 90 indigenous	Iraqi documentation; out of 120 imported warheads, 92 were 'conventional' and 28 'special'; out of 90 indigenous warheads 73 were 'conventional' and 17 'special'

attack on Iraq's southern neighbour. Once there, Brigade 223 trained for the deployment of its al-Husseins from fixed launchers and its older MAZ-543 TELs, while Brigade 224 was busy pre-selecting and measuring alternative firing sites and camouflaging its an-Nidaas in the desert. Both units were heavily protected: a total of six battalions equipped with Soviet-made 2K12 Kub mobile SAMs (ASCC/NATO codename 'SA-6 Gainful') were deployed in their support. Meanwhile, Ayyubi took care to evacuate all the available al-Hussein and Laith missiles from their usual depot at al-Iskandariya, outside Kerbala, and to hide them at various places around western Iraq.

The SSMD did not take part in actions in Kuwait of 2–4 August, but immediately after ran its next wargame simulating attacks on Israel. In October 1990, the Directorate of Operations of the Iraqi Armed Forces drew up a new plan for a massive strike upon Israel. Based on intelligence collected by Mirage F.1EQ-5s in 1989, this envisaged including more than 50 combat aircraft – including all 30 of the brand-new Su-24MKs available by the time, which were to punch a hole in the Israeli air defences with the help of Soviet-made Kh-58 anti-radiation missiles (ASCC/NATO codename 'AS-11 Kilter'). The SSMD was then to follow up with al-Hussein missiles. At least one related exercise was undertaken later the same month. On 2 November 1990, the sole Faw-727 started flying regular sorties along the border with Saudi Arabia and MiG-25s followed up with several shallow penetrations of Saudi airspace. On 16 November, the sole Adnan-2 airborne early warning aircraft flew a sortie close to the Saudi border, and on 2 December it made another sortie deep into Jordanian airspace. The exact purpose and results of this activity remain unclear, but it is possible that they tested enemy reaction times and served to familiarise the crews involved with potential areas of operation – as well as that, at least some of the resulting intelligence was forwarded to the SSMD via the GMID.

By 15 January 1991, the SSMD was organised as listed in Table 3, and had a total of four al-Wallid TELs with Brigade 223; 10 MAZ-543 TELs with Brigade 224 and 28 fixed launchers positioned in western Iraq. One semi-trailer launcher used for training, and two al-Wallids and another semi-trailer launcher used for experimental purposes were kept back at Camp Taji, together with 50 flatbed trailers acquired for the construction of additional mobile launchers. A further 28 fixed launchers were manufactured by this time, and were ready for deployment, but never brought into position. One possible reason is that for this total of 56 fixed launchers, the SSMD had only 24 functional control panels.

While the mass of warheads for available al-Husseins were conventional, those for al-Hijarass were made of concrete. Moreover, by January 1991, the Iraqis had constructed 25 warheads for biological weapons trials, five for chemical weapons trials, and manufactured another 80 for chemical weapons. Indeed,

such warheads were supplied to both Brigade 223 and 224, and their commanders were authorised to deploy them in the event of the US, Coalition, or Israeli forces deploying nuclear weapons against Iraq.

MODIFIED FLOGGERS[4]

Through the second half of 1990, as it became obvious that Iraq was heading for a collision with the US-led Coalition, the IrAF intensified its own preparations for the coming show-down. At least four projects including modifications of Soviet aircraft with French-made avionics and other equipment are known to have been undertaken during that period. The first two of them addressed the lack of self-protection electronic warfare systems on MiG-23ML and MiG-29 interceptors of the IrAF. During the last two years of the war with Iran, Iraqi Mirage F.1EQs were equipped with

This still from a video shows an AM.39 Exocet (and its large launch rail) installed on MiG-23ML serial number 23252. This adaptation proved unviable because the Exocet required a very unusual power supply system for powering-up prior to release, and this proved much too cumbersome for installation into the MiG. (Tom Cooper collection)

Port-view of the MiG-23ML serial number 23298, showing the R-24 missile (foreground, top), and – in the lower left corner – the rear part of the Remora pod and its pylon. (Tom Cooper collection)

TMV-002 Remora jammers, and these had proved effective in at least disturbing the work of the powerful AWG-9 radar and fire-control system of the F-14A Tomcat. Moreover, the installation of Remora required a bare minimum of modifications because the pod was autonomous: it came together with a pylon containing the necessary power supply and cooling/heating systems. After a slight redesign of the pylon, Remoras were installed instead of the port under-fuselage hardpoint – used for R-60 air-to-air missiles (ASCC/NATO codename 'AA-8 Aphid') – on a handful of MiG-23MLs from No. 73 Squadron. They and most of the other MiG-23MLs of Nos 73 and 93 Squadron also received SPO-15 Beryoza radar warning receivers and ASO-2 chaff and flare dispensers, usually installed on Su-22M-4s.

Less successful was the attempt to adapt MiG-23MLs for the deployment of AM.39 Exocet anti-ship missiles: although the aircraft with serial number 23252 (from No. 73 Squadron) was modified to carry the hefty launch rail and the missile under the centreline,

the installation of the unique power supply for this weapon proved much too complex and this project was eventually abandoned. Finally, a few MiG-23BNs of No. 49 Squadron (known are serials 23163 and 23173) and two Su-22M-4s were modified through the addition of French-made in-flight refuelling probes on the right side of the upper front fuselage, and the necessary plumbing. This modification was flight tested, and retained, but never employed in operations.

FULCRUMS WITH REMORA[5]

The successful installation of Remora on the MiG-23ML gave birth to the idea to attempt something similar with much more modern MiG-29s of which Iraq had originally placed an order for 137 examples. With Moscow in need of hard currency following the Chernobyl catastrophe, their deliveries began in late 1986. As far as is known, 39 were delivered by the time Baghdad stopped further procurement in early 1990. The reason was that the Iraqis found their avionics lagging behind those of Mirage F.1EQ-6s, and that the Soviets had failed to deliver such weapons as the R-27T (IR-homing variant of what the ASCC/NATO codenamed the 'AA-10 Alamo') and R-73E ('AA-11 Archer'). Therefore, the IrAF opted to continue with purchases of the much more powerful Sukhoi Su-27 instead. Negotiations for that order were interrupted by the invasion of Kuwait and the resulting arms embargo imposed by the UN.

Meanwhile, the MiG-29s that were accepted by Iraq entered service with Nos. 6 and 39 Squadrons, of which the former was officially declared operational in April 1988: the latter was still working-up as of late 1990. Not to be outdone, once the Kuwait crisis erupted,

A particularly useful view of the underside of one of the modified 'Iraqi Fulcrums' (IrAF serial number 29062; construction number 22994), taken after the jet was captured by US Marines in 2003. Note the 'empty' holders for the inboard underwing hardpoints; launch rails for R-27 missiles that had been moved to the centre underwing position, and the outboard underwing hardpoint (on the left side) with its usual R-60 launch rail. (Tom Cooper collection)

A semi-profile of a modified 'Iraqi Fulcrum' (serial number 29040, construction number 21830), seen after its capture by US troops, at the former Tammuz AB in 2006. Notable is that the launch rail for R-27 missiles was moved from its usual inboard underwing position to the central underwing position. (Tom Cooper collection)

the IrAF went to some lengths to lessen the vulnerability of the MiG-29's weapons system through modifications. On at least two examples, the inboard underwing pylons were removed and plumed to accept a drop tank on the right/starboard side, and the Remora jammer on the left/port side. In turn, launch rails for R-27R missiles – usually installed on inboard underwing stations – were moved to the centre position. Only the outboard underwing pylons – usually carrying R-60 missiles – were retained in their place. The resulting 'Iraqi Fulcrum' was thus limited to carrying a total of four missiles instead of the usual six, but had much better protection against enemy interceptors, which it was to prove in combat in 1991.

IN ACTION

The US-led Coalition opened its aerial onslaught early on 16 January 1991, with an all-out effort against the Kari IADS. The Iraqis promptly responded with fire from the two brigades of the SSMD equipped with tactical ballistic missiles. Together, Brigades 225 and 226 fired 45 Ababil-50 and SS-30 rockets, and three Laith-90s during the night of 16 to 17 January, and another 30 SS-30 and Laith-90 rockets the night after – all at Coalition positions south of Kuwait, and with unknown results. The airpower of the US-led alliance was initially busy demolishing the Kari system, but on 17 January it hit the workshops of Team 144/2 in Camp Taji. This prompted Saddam to order the rest of the SSMD into action against Israel, though with conventional warheads only. Early on 18 January 1991, Brigade 224 fired eight al-Hussein missiles from well-dispersed positions in 'Zone 4', in the western desert. Targets were military factories selected from 32 folders prepared by the GMID, and also the city of Tel Aviv. Brigade 223 attempted to follow in fashion but its effort to launch an al-Hussein from one of its an-Wallid TELs failed. With Israel not being protected by any of the MIM-104 Patriot PAC-1/2 SAM systems at the time, at least two missiles that did work hit Tel Aviv, one crashing into Azor, and the other in the Ezra district. Due to the comprehensive civil protection measures of the Israeli authorities, there were no fatalities, but 22 people were injured. Late the same day, Brigades 225 and 226 fired their last known volleys, including 13 SS-30s and Laith-90s: once again, results remained unknown.

Early on 19 January 1991, Brigade 224 fired four additional al-Husseins at Tel Aviv, three of which hit the city, causing material damage only, while one crashed into the Mediterranean Sea. Meanwhile, Brigade 223 was redeployed to the Basra area with instructions to commence action against Saudi Arabia. In the case of that country, proclaimed targets included both civilian and military facilities – primarily the sprawling Dhahran Air Base. Late on 20 January 1991, the unit fired two al-Husseins at Dhahran: the town and nearby military bases were protected by PAC-2 SAM sites that fired five missiles in return and claimed two 'Scuds' as shot down. Debris is known to have fallen near the barracks of the US Army component with the Central Command, a Saudi police camp, and the port, but without causing damage.

By 21 January, Brigade 223 managed to make all four of its an-Wallid TELs operational and fired four al-Husseins at Saudi Arabia; two at Dhahran and two in the direction of Riyadh. Patriot SAM sites fired 26 missiles (eight at the first incoming missile and six at each of those following) and claimed a total of 14 kills. Only one Iraqi missile actually caused any kind

The night skies of Tel Aviv, on 12 February 1991, showing several Patriot SAMs in the process of intercepting an incoming al-Hussein Mod. (GPO)

This still is from a training video taken in the USA showing one of the MAZ-543/9P119 TELs that the USA obtained in the 1990s and is closely reminiscent of Brigade 224's operations during the war of 1991. Vehicles of this unit spent most of the war well-hidden in the desert; the missiles were prepared for deployment during the night, and then quickly brought into firing position. (US DoD)

of damage: it blew out the back wall of a building, producing a crater about three metres in diameter, and wounded 12 people. A day later, Brigade 223 – now reinforced by part of Brigade 224, redeployed to bolster this effort – repeated the exercise by firing another two missiles at Riyadh and two at Dhahran. Patriot SAM sites protecting the Saudi capital fired 30 interceptors in return, claiming both 'Scuds' as shot down, though a nearly intact body of one Scud is known to have hit an empty road. In the Dhahran area, one al-Hussein passed the zone defended by PAC SAMs, and hit the desert about 80km west of the town,

The fuselage of an al-Hussein Mod that came down in Saudi Arabia in January 1991. Notably, the heat at re-entry (and, possible combat damage), have melted parts of the sand paint, revealing its original, dark green colour. (US DoD)

while another was claimed as shot down into the water of the Gulf, north of Qatar: nevertheless, its debris is known to have hit Dhahran Air Base shortly after a Coalition aircraft took off.

Late on 23 January, the SSMD fired five missiles within a very short time, including one at Israel, two at Riyadh and two at Dhahran. This prompted an active response from the Patriot SAMs, which claimed at least three as shot down: subsequent investigation revealed that several of the interceptors were fired at false targets. On the evening of 25 January, two al-Husseins approached Riyadh: the PAC SAM sites fired a total of four missiles, claiming both as shot down, but one completely demolished a six story building of the Department of Interior in the downtown (about 2,000 metres from the Ministry of Defence and Aviation housing the CENTCOM Headquarters), killing one person and injuring 30.

An al-Hussein Mod warhead that came down in Saudi Arabia on 17 February 1991. (US DoD)

Table 6: Iraqi Missile Attacks against Israel, Saudi Arabia, Bahrain and Qatar, 1991				
Date	Local Time	Missiles	Target	Notes
16 January	unknown	45x SS-30	unknown	fired into Saudi Arabia, damage unknown
16 January	unknown	3x Laith	unknown	fired into Saudi Arabia, damage unknown
17 January	unknown	30x SS-30 & Laith	unknown	fired into Saudi Arabia, damage unknown
18 January	unknown	13x SS-30 & Laith	unknow	fired into Saudi Arabia, damage unknown
18 January	0200 hrs	2x Hussein	Tel Aviv	hit Azor and Ezra districts, 22 injuries
19 January	0715 hrs	4x Hussein	Tel Aviv	3 hit Hatkiva and Ezra districts, and Yarkon Park (1 failed to detonate), 1 crashed into the sea south of Tel Aviv
20 January	2143 hrs	2x Hussein	Dhahran	2 shot down by PAC
21 January	0042 hrs	2x Hussein	Riyadh	2 shot down by PAC, debris hit an office building
21 January	1229 hrs	2x Hussein	Dhahran	1 shot down by PAC, debris hit runway of Dhahran IAP; 1 hit water
21 January	2218 hrs	1x Hussein	al-Jubayl	no damage
22 January	0341 hrs	3x Hussein	Riyadh	3 shot down by PAC, debris hit an empty road
22 January	0710 hrs	3x Hussein	Dhahran	2 missed, 1 shot down
22 January	2040 hrs	1x Hussein	Tel Aviv	hit Ramat Gan, killed 3 (two to heart attacks), injured 84
23 January	2220 hrs	1x Hussein	Haifa	1 shot down, debris fell into water
23 January	2254 hrs	2x Hussein	Dhahran	1 shot down, debris fell within and outside US base
23 January	2254 hrs	2x Hussein	Riyadh	2 shot down

(Table 6 continued overleaf)

Table 6: Iraqi Missile Attacks against Israel, Saudi Arabia, Bahrain and Qatar, 1991 *(continued)*				
25 January	2223 hrs	2x Hussein	Riyadh	1 shot down, other hit Department of Interior building, killing 1, injuring 30
25 January	1800 hrs	5–6x Hussein	Tel Aviv	3 hit Ramat Hataysim, Ramat Gan and near Hamaccabia Stadium, killed 1, injured 67
25 January	1800 hrs	1x Hussein	Haifa	no damage
26 January	0328 hrs	1x Hussein	Dhahran	1 shot down, debris hit runway of Dhahran IAP
26 January	2200 hrs	3x Hussein	Tel Aviv	no damage
26 January	2200 hrs	1x Hussein	Haifa	no damage
26 January	2246 hrs	1x Hussein	Riyadh	missed CENTCOM HQ by 400 metres
28 January	2055 hrs	1x Hussein	Riyadh	1 shot down, debris hit farm in suburbs without causing damage
28 January	2100 hrs	1x Hussein	Tel Aviv	crashed near Dir Balut, West Bank, no damage
31 January	1900 hrs	1x Hussein	Tel Aviv	crashed in the Samaria area, no damage
2 February	2030 hrs	1x Hussein	Tel Aviv	crashed in West Bank, no damage
3 February	0041 hrs	1x Hussein	Riyadh	detonated near apartment building, injuring 29
3 February	0140 hrs	1x Hussein	Tel Aviv	crashed in West Bank, no damage
8 February	0154 hrs	1x Hussein	Riyadh	1 shot down but warhead hit parking lot
9 February	0240 hrs	1x Hussein	Tel Aviv	hit Ramat Gan, causing extensive material damage, 13 injured
11 February	1900 hrs	1x Hussein	Tel Aviv	hit the sea north of Tel Aviv, no damage
11 February	2220 hrs	1x Hussein	Riyadh	1 shot down, warhead hit Islamic University causing significant material damage
12 February	0130 hrs	1x Hussein	Tel Aviv	hit Sayyon, demolished two and badly damaged other homes, 9 injured
14 February	1145 hrs	2x Hussein	KKMC	damaged a building in Hafr al-Batin
16 February	0201 hrs	1x Hussein	al-Jubayl	hit water near ammunition depot
16 February	2010 hrs	1x Hussein	Haifa	crashed in water
16 February	2010 hrs	3x Hussein	Dimona	al-Hijara; no damage
19 February	1950 hrs	1x Hussein	Tel Aviv	1 shot down, crashed 7–11km east of Ben Gurion IAP, no damage
21 February	1706 hrs	2x Hussein	KKMC	no damage
21 February	2100 hrs	1x Hussein	KKMC	no damage
22 February	0231 hrs	3x Hussein	Bahrain	1 shot down
23 February	0459 hrs	2x Hussein	Dhahran	missed King Fahd IAP by 20km, other broke up in flight
23 February	1840 hrs	1x Hussein	Tel Aviv	no damage
24 February	0432 hrs	1x Hussein	Riyadh	1 shot down but warhead hit school causing material damage
24 February	1217 hrs	1x Hussein	KKMC	1 shot down
24 February	2123 hrs	1x Hussein	Riyadh	possibly shot down, broke up before or as a result of intercept
25 February	2032 hrs	1x Hussein	Dhahran	hit US barrack killing 28 and injuring over 100
25 February	0340 hrs	1x Hussein	Dimona	no damage
25 February	0540 hrs	1x Hussein	Dimona	no damage
26 February	0126 hrs	1x Hussein	Qatar	overflew Dhahran, fell 70km short of Doha

Starting with 14 February, Iraq began targeting the huge King Khalid Military City (KKMC) in the Hafr al-Batin area. Following careful preparation during the night (all missiles were always prepared under the cover of darkness), two al-Husseins were fired at this installation in the middle of the day, from two different launch locations. The PAC-2 SAM site protecting it did not engage, and thus one al-Hussein badly damaged a home and destroyed five or six cars in the southeast of Hafr al-Batin, while the other hit an empty spot in another apartment block, causing minor damage only, and injuring four people. Early on 16 February, Iraq launched a single al-Hussein at the port of al-Jubayl: the Patriot SAM site protecting the town and nearby military facilities was undergoing maintenance and could not engage. The missile thus went on to hit the water in the port, near a large pier where six ships and two smaller craft were tied up.

The strike on the KKMC of 21 February was launched from the Baghdad area during the evening: both missiles were engaged by Patriots but these failed to hit, and al-Husseins fell into an empty area. On the same day, a Laith-90 fired by Brigade 225, narrowly missed one of the bases of the Senegalese troops deployed in Saudi

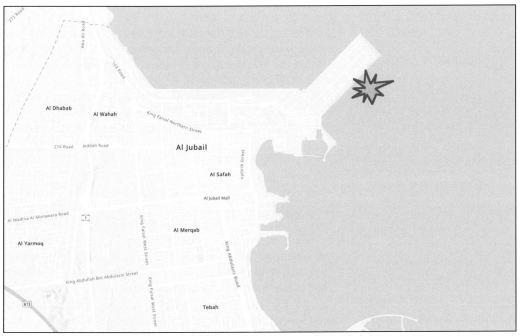

A map of the port of Jubayl with impact of the al-Hussein of 16 February 1991. (US DoD)

examination resulted in the counting of 97, of which 88 hit the areas under the control of the US-led Coalition, Israel, or their neighbourhood: 46 of these against Saudi Arabia and Qatar, and 41 or 42 in or near Israel. Precise Iraqi figures became available over a decade ago and confirmed the launch of 43 missiles at Israel. Of these, 39 fell on Israeli territory – or the waters of the Mediterranean Sea nearby – and three in the West Bank. As far as is known, they caused the direct death of two persons (additionally, seven people suffocated due to improper use of gas masks and five fatal heart attacks were attributed to Iraqi strikes), and injured 815 (of whom 230 directly).[7] Another 50 missiles were fired on targets in Saudi Arabia, Bahrain and Qatar.

Arabia along with a 30,000-strong contingent from eight other Islamic nations: eight Senegalese were wounded as a result.[6]

The most successful Iraqi missile strike took place in the evening of 25 February, when a single al-Hussein was launched in the direction of Dhahran. Although the town and nearby facilities were protected by two SAM sites, one was down for maintenance, while the other suffered software problems. The warhead hit a warehouse in the Aujan compound of the al-Khobar suburb that served as US Army barracks, killing 28 troops from the 475th Quartermaster Group (a reservist unit), and injuring more than 100 (about half of them seriously).

STATISTICS

The total number of al-Husseins, al-Hijaras, Laiths and other rockets fired by Iraq during the war of 1991 was initially unknown and a matter of significant dispute between Western historians, with some claiming as many as 344 firings. A detailed post-war cross-

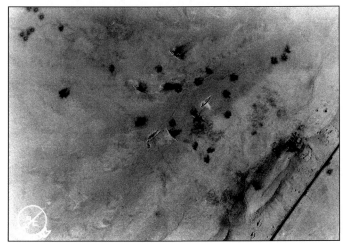

A reconnaissance photograph taken by a TARPS reconnaissance pod carried by an F-14A of fighter squadron VF-32 'Swordsmen' (embarked on the aircraft carrier USS *John F Kennedy*, CV-67) during the war of 1991, showing suspected trenches hiding MAZ-543/9P117 TELs of Brigade 224. As can be seen from the scorch marks on the ground, this position was heavily bombed, and several trenches received direct hits, destroying the vehicles inside. However, none of the vehicles in question were TELs (nor trailers) of Brigades 223 and 224. (US Navy Photo)

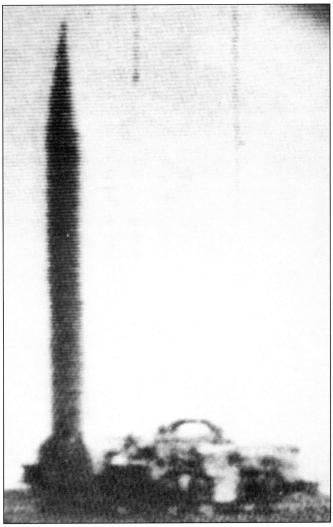

A still from a video released by Iraqi National TV, showing an al-Hussein missile in the erected position, shortly before being fired, in 1991. (Tom Cooper collection)

Table 7: Iraqi R-17 and al-Hussein Expenditure, 1976–1991[8]

Expenditure	Declared Quantity	Source
pre-1980 training	8	Iraqi documentation
Iran–Iraq War, 1980-1988	516	Iraqi documentation & independent sources
testing, 1985-1990	69	Iraqi documentation & independent sources
Gulf War, 1991	93	Iraqi documentation & independent sources
destruction under SCR 687, July 1991	48	UNSCOM verification
unilateral destruction, July–October 1991	86	Iraqi documentation

Gradually, the reasons for such large discrepancies were explained as due to erroneous information, double- or triple reporting of the same missile strikes, false targets caused by radar interference and the fact that the warhead of the al-Hussein Mod separated from the fuselage, that al-Husseins tended to break up into multiple parts upon re-entry into the atmosphere, and other factors. As far as is known, the radars of PAC-1/2 SAM systems detected 88 al-Husseins, but engaged only the 51 that entered areas protected by them: 36 were claimed as intercepted and 27 were claimed as shot down – in the sense of their warhead being destroyed or the missile fuselage being knocked off course. In turn, the US and allies flew up to 500 sorties in attempt to find and destroy the Iraqi TELs, but only once found one of the 9P117s, and failed to knock out even one of the 28 fixed launchers in the western desert, although striking them repeatedly.

In turn, although launching the 'Big Scud Hunt', and flying 200-500 reconnaissance and combat sorties a day, and claiming a number of TELs and all fixed launchers to have been destroyed, the Coalition failed to knock out even one. Contemporary means of reconnaissance and command and control were much too slow to enable 24/7 coverage over even the most-relevant parts of Iraq. Thus, even if one or another of Brigade 224's MAZ-543s was captured on reconnaissance photographs of US and British aircraft, they were always well away and hidden by the time strike aircraft could reach the scene.

12
RECOVERY AND DEMISE

During ceasefire negotiations that ended the war of 1991, the US-led Coalition demanded the unconditional destruction of all of Iraq's weapons of mass destruction. Grudgingly, Baghdad agreed and, in accordance with the United Nations Security Council's Resolution 687 of April 1991, let the inspectors of the United Nations Special Commission (UNSCOM) into the country. Between 14 April 1991 and 14 August 1991, UNSCOM inspectors supervised the destruction of 63 ballistic missiles (including 48 al-Husseins), 50 warheads, six 9P119/MAZ-543 and two al-Wallid TELs. Furthermore, the UN inspectors supervised the destruction of a solid-propellant mixer acquired as part of Project 235/Badr-2000. However, because they had been provided with the serial numbers of all the R-17Es that Moscow had exported to Baghdad, the inspectors knew that there were many more left. Therefore, inspections were continued, while the SSMD attempted to hide the remaining missiles at different sites in central and southern Iraq. Then, in early 1992, Saddam Hussein – keen to rid Iraq of sanctions – issued an order for the destruction of all the missiles and for their wreckage to be handed over to UNSCOM. By then, relations were damaged to the degree where nobody trusted Iraq anymore. This is why the USA and its allies continued insisting on related UN inspections for the next 11 years.

UNSCOM INSPECTIONS
While prohibiting production and operational deployment of weapons of mass destruction (WMD), Resolution 687 granted Iraq permission to develop and operate missiles with range of 150km. Always concerned by Iranian intentions, and emphasising the need to recover as much as possible of the defence industry that was badly damaged by US and allied air strikes, Saddam reorganised the SSMRD into the Authority for Scientific and Technical Research and Development of the Armed Forces, and appointed Saadi at its director. The latter then focused all of his and his team's attention and efforts into two types of projects, both essentially based on the technology Iraq already possessed and knew well; liquid-fuelled missiles based on the technology of the S-75 Dvina SAM; and Solid-fuelled missiles based on the technology of the M-87 Orkan/Ababil-50.

Initiated in August 1991 with the aim of obtaining a weapon that could deliver a payload of 300kg over a range of 150km, the new liquid-fuelled missile was codenamed G-1. It was based on experience with the former Project Fahad-300/500, using the engine of the Soviet-made V-750 surface-to-air missile, and developed by a team led by Dr. Hamid Khalil al-Azzawi and General Ra'ad Ismail Jamil al-Adhami Ibn al-Haytham. The first prototype – named ar-Rafadiyan – failed during the testing 1992, but the work went on as Azzawi and Haytham expanded its fuselage to 500mm diameter. In January–April 1993, several successful flight tests were undertaken, during one of which the missile reached the range of 162km, while missing its target by just 40 metres. Encouraged, later the same year, Tamimi – now Director of the SSMRD – proposed a redesign with diameter of 750mm, but the UNSCOM, which closely monitored all the activity, restricted the diameter to 600mm. A year later, the entire project was reviewed by Hussein Kamil, who selected General Haytham's design, now renamed as-Samoud.

In 1995, Hussein Kamil – now not only the Chief of the MIMI, but also Saddam's son-in-law – defected to Jordan. When interviewed by the Americans, he admitted that Iraq had concealed two al-Hussein missiles and associated equipment from the UN. Arguably, his claim could not be verified by the UNSCOM, and Baghdad insisted that all the missiles and TELs had been destroyed. But, because of his defection, Saddam ordered an end to all work related to missiles with a range longer than 150km. In place of Hussein Kamil, Saddam appointed Abd at-Tawab Abdallah al-Mullah Huwaysh as the new Minister of Military Industry. The change at the top resulted in little improvement of the original Samoud design: marred by issues related to its poor stability, it remained unsuccessful.

RECOVERY
The flight testing of the Samoud was continued through 1997, still under the supervision of UNSCOM until Saddam grew impatient and issued orders for the latter to be refused access to various sites. Eventually, the administration of President Bill Clinton then withdrew inspectors and, on 16–19 December 1998, launched Operation Desert Fox, conducted in cooperation with Great Britain.

A test launch of an early version of the Samoud in 1997. Notable is the TEL, constructed on the chassis of a Yugoslav-made FAP 3232 truck. (Ali Tobchi collection)

Intended to destabilise the Iraqi government, Desert Fox included airstrikes and cruise missile attacks against 97 targets – mostly military bases, storage facilities, surface-to-air batteries, air bases, and weapons production facilities. Enraged, Saddam decided to cease cooperation with UNSCOM and ordered an acceleration of the missile programs. Early the following year, General Haytham was removed, and Huwaysh appointed Tamimi as director of Project Samoud. However, the Iraqi engineer and his team never found a workable solution and the project was cancelled in 2000.

Meanwhile, the SSMRD launched work on constructing new infrastructure, and repairing the old, for development of long-ranged weapons, including a new test stand for liquid-propelled engines much larger and more capable than anything previously available. Thanks to the new facilities, the team developed and tested the new liquid propellant AZ-11, which demonstrated significant improvement in performance during a test run on 18 March 2001. Making use of such infrastructure, in June 2001, Huwaysh launched Project as-Samoud II, aiming to develop a missile with a range beyond the 150-kilometre limit imposed by the UN. This time, he opted for a diameter of 760mm in order to enable the use of components taken from HY-2 missiles, and to make enough space for a larger fuel tank. Manufactured in the al-Karma factory, the Samoud II proved highly precise: during flight tests, it achieved a CEP of just 40 metres. Series production was carried out at the al-Karma factory, which rolled out the first batch of 62 missiles, before launching work on the second batch in February 2002.

PROJECT FATH, TAKE II

While Huwaysh was working on Samoud, and then Samoud II, another team initiated the work on a version of the same design equipped with a solid-fuel motor (sometimes called 'al-Ubur'). This was expected to reach a range of over 200km. Thanks to repairs on one of two mixers and both bowls left from the Badr-2000 project, 'disabled' by the UNSCOM in 1991, and construction of an annealing chamber capable of handling solid-fuel motor cases with a diameter of 700–1,000mm and more, and the repairs at the al-Musayyib Solid Rocket Motor Support and Test Facility, at al-Mutasim, the project advanced quite rapidly.

The Fath had very simply construction: it was 6.7m long, had a fin-span of 1.4m, and weighed 1,200kg, of which 770–856kg was its solid-fuel motor. While heavy, its airframe was made of the same material as the rocket motor casing, thus greatly easing development and production. The Fath was actually an unguided missile – it used stabilisation fins positioned aft – and it was designed for deployment from the SM-90 launcher of the SA-2 SAM system. The whole was made mobile with the help of four LRSV-262 firing units and four FAP 3232 trucks carrying reloads of the Ababil-50 system: two of the latter had SM-90 launchers mounted on their flatbeds, thus becoming the primary TELs for the Faths – which in turn resulted in these becoming colloquially known as 'Ababil-100'. In turn, while at this work, the Iraqis took care not only to extend the shelf-life of the remaining Ababil-50 rockets by replacing their original motors with newly-made ones including composite solid-propellants (Project an-Nida), but also removed the original launchers from the LRSV-262s and replaced them with SM-90 launchers, atop of which only six tubes were installed (instead of the original 12). In this fashion, the total number of available launchers for Fath/Ababil-100 and Ababil-50 was increased to eight.

Carried out between early 2000 and late 2002, testing included 17 static motor tests and 33 flight tests, and proved consistent range performance – but not consistent reliability and precision: up to 30 percent of the missiles failed upon launch and they never achieved the desired CEP of 750 metres. Nevertheless, it was a relatively simple weapon that could be made in numbers with the use of the available equipment, and it proved capable of exceeding

A modified LRSV-262 firing unit from the M-87 Orkan/Ababil system, captured by US troops in 2003. Notably, the Iraqis replaced the original mount with a SM-90 launcher from the S-75 SAM system, and then fixed six launch tubes atop of its swivelling arm. (via Ali Tobchi)

An al-Samoud missile on display during a military parade in Baghdad in 2000. The final design was strongly influenced by the experience of re-manufacturing al-Hussein missiles from R-17Es. (via Ali Tobchi)

A still from a video taken during a military parade in Baghdad in 2000, showing an Ababil-100 system, including a modified LRSV-262 firing unit with SM-90 launcher, along with the missile. (Ali Tobchi collection)

It was armed by a sustained acceleration of 7.5gs for a duration of at least 2.5 seconds, and equipped with a contact fuse. The other was a CBU type, essentially a 3mm thick shell case made of aluminium, filled with 850–900 KB-1 bomblets from old SRS-262 rockets of the M-87 Orkan/Ababil-50. These were stacked atop each other and held in place by foam moulds. Originally, the CBU warhead was released with a barometric sensor and explosive cord. When the missile ascended to an altitude of 5,500 metres, a thermal battery connected, charging the capacitors within the firing circuit; when it descended to an altitude of 3,000 metres, the capacitor discharged power to the detonator, which then initiated the detonation cord: the latter then fragmented the warhead and let the airstream disperse the bomblets. In practice, this meant that the bomblets were released from an altitude of 1,500–2,000 metres, which was actually below what was desirable.

Five static tests were undertaken to test the function of the CBU warhead, of which three were successful, indicating necessity for improvement. Therefore, between April and August 2002, a new design was developed using – in addition to the detonator cord necessary to fracture the casing – a single charge positioned in the centre of the warhead to bolster the dispersion of the bomblets. Apparently, this solution proved unsatisfactory and the explosive charge was removed. Furthermore, the Iraqis replaced the barometric fuse with a diaphragm switch powered by a battery from Ababil-50 rockets. No unconventional warheads were ever developed for either Samoud II or the Fath.

Despite delays with the procurement of guidance and control systems, the Iraqis eventually obtained the necessary equipment and carried out two guided flight tests of the Fath: one with roll control and the other with pitch control. Indeed, as of March 2003, the SSMRD was only weeks from conducting a test with the full control system, including INS and canards. The engineers involved remain convinced that, had they been left to complete their work, it would have given them an opportunity to validate that their concept worked.

the UN-imposed limit of 150km during one of its early tests (when the missile came down 161km away from its launch point). Furthermore, it promised to become even more capable once the Iraqis added a guidance system, as they hoped for, right from the start. Through the late 1990s, Baghdad had repeatedly attempted to acquire inertial guidance systems, and control components from the former Yugoslavia and the USSR.

Arguably, the series production of the Fath was marred by several issues. Because of the insufficient capacity of the two available bowls, the Iraqis used four smaller, 30-gallon bowls and two mixers to mix the propellant for one motor. While still liquid the propellant was then poured into the motor casing. This procedure proved unsatisfactory for it eliminated the option of simultaneous casting of multiple motors and resulted in inconsistent motor performance – including several in-flight disintegrations.

Two types of warheads were developed for the Fath: one was the classic, unitary high-explosive type, having a mass of between 260kg and 300kg, and containing between 160kg and 170kg of explosive.

AIR FORCE PROJECTS

The infrastructure of the IrAF was savaged by the war of 1991. Moreover, immediately afterwards the UN authorised the establishment of two no-fly zones (NFZs) over Iraq; the northern extended from the 36th parallel to the Turkish border; and the southern was south of the 32nd parallel, but, in 1996, expanded to the 33rd parallel.

Reminiscent of the 'air policing' by the RAF and the Royal Iraqi Air Force of the 1920s and the 1930s, both NFZs were maintained exclusively through air power: the northern by aircraft operating from NATO's air bases in Turkey, and the southern by aircraft operating from air bases in Kuwait, Saudi Arabia, and aircraft carriers underway in the Persian Gulf. The establishment of the two NFZs meant that the IrAF lost the services of about a dozen major air bases: it was only able to evacuate equipment that survived the war of 1991 from them.

Initially, the Iraqis did not challenge the NFZ, but this began to change in 1992, when IrAF did try to disrupt some related operations. After losing two fighter jets in resulting air combats, and due to the declining state of its interceptor fleet, for the next eight years the air force limited the activity of its fleet. Remaining MiG-21s and MiG-29s were withdrawn from service in 1994–1995 because both fleets were experiencing growing issues with their engines, and airframes were beyond their flying hours, while the IrAF still lacked capacity to overhaul them at home. Thus, the entire interceptor fleet was downsized to two squadrons of MiG-23s, one squadron of MiG-25s, and two of Mirage F.1EQs. Even then, many of the about 50 remaining airframes required overhauls and upgrades to remain operational or retain any kind of operational value. Attempting to do that with tools and equipment that survived 1991, the IrAF achieved mixed results.

During the first half of the 1990s, the solid-fuel motors of Matra R.550 Magic Mk.I missiles exceed their shelf-life. Technicians of No. 89 Squadron attempted to replace them by installing Soviet-made R-60 missiles on the wingtip stations of at least one Mirage F.1EQ-6. While the necessary rewiring proved no particular problem, one missile malfunctioned shortly after launch during flight testing and fell harmlessly to the ground. After this experience, the commanding officer No. 89 Squadron – always anything but optimistic about installing a Soviet-made missile onto one of his jets – ordered a halt to related work. Eventually, the MIC solved this issue by launching domestic production of solid motors, not only for R.550s, but also for Matra Super 530Fs. Both the R.550 and Super 530F were then successfully flight tested and test launched from a Mirage F.1EQ-6 of No. 89 Squadron, and then the entire stock of missiles of French origin received new motors.

While the number of fully mission capable MiG-23MLs, MiG-25PD (export)s and Mirage F.1EQs was kept stable for much of the 1990s, they proved increasingly unable to challenge the continuously improved variants of US and British interceptors pressed into service during the decade. The IrAF eventually concluded that its actual primary opponents were early warning aircraft, such as the Grumman E-2C Hawkeye of the US Navy, and Boeing E-3 Sentry of the US Air Force and the Royal Air Force. This drove the Iraqis to search for a solution to combat such aircraft. In 1998, a team of engineers led by Colonel Hamza came up with the idea to modify a surviving MiG-25RB reconnaissance-strike fighter by installing Fantasmagoria anti-radiation targeting pods and Kh-58 anti-radiation missiles left over from the IrAF fleet of Su-24MK fighter-bombers. One MiG was brought to a maintenance hangar of Taqaddum AB and stripped of its reconnaissance camera system to make space for parts of the Fantasmagoria. For unknown reasons – said to have been related to Operation Desert Fox – this project was eventually abandoned.

RUSHDIE SYSTEM

Another idea born around the same time was to deploy the Soviet-made BM-21 Grad multiple rocket system for air defence purposes. In 1999, Ali al-Tobchi, one of the engineers working at the Taji complex, arrived at this idea based on the range of the BM-21's 9M28F rockets. Equipped with fragmentation warheads and the usual contact fuse, these had a maximum horizontal range of 15,000 metres. But, if equipped with a barometric fuse, they could be set up to detonate at pre-selected altitudes, all the way up to 11,000 metres. Tobchi explained this to his director but apparently nothing happened. It was only four months later that he was informed of the result. In a project led by Brigadier General Ahmad Sadik Rushdie al-Astrabadi, the workshops of the IrAF used the mount of the Czechoslovak-made M53 30mm anti-aircraft gun (better known as 30-2 in Iraq): they removed the gun and instead installed two tubes for BM-21 rockets equipped with barometric fuses. Testing of the resulting weapons system was conducted against US and British aircraft maintaining the NFZ over southern Iraq. The unit equipped with the new weapons was designated 'Rushdie System', and reported its rockets had detonated near several incoming aircraft, causing them all to promptly turn back south, and return to Saudi Arabia. The Rushdie System remained in service and was credited with downing a Boeing AH-64 Apache attack helicopter of the US Army, near Karbala, on 22 March 2003.

Another improvisation that emerged around the same time was related to the Soviet-made S-125 SAM system ('SA-3 Goa') – and

A still from a video released by the US Department of Defense showing one of the earliest SA-3 modifications of 1999–2002, including a twin-rail launcher mounted on a commercial trailer. (US DoD)

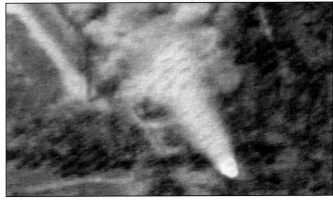

Missile Battery 232 included some of the most skilled Iraqi operators of mobile SA-3 SAM systems. In addition to downing several UAVs, in 1999 it managed to damage a General Dynamics/Lockheed-Martin F-16C of the US Air Force with a visually guided V-601 missile equipped with a booster-section from V755 or V-759, in a scene similar to this. (US DoD)

went into two directions. One was to mobilise this system, every battery of which included four heavy and cumbersome, quadruple launchers. The initial idea was to mount the entire launcher on a standard, 13.6m-long truck-towed commercial trailer. This proved promising but was still too cumbersome. Instead, a solution was found in removing launch rails from their original launchers and installing two of them on the flatbed of an Isuzu light truck, imported from Japan: the SRN-125 fire-control radar was installed on a bigger trailer. Another modification aimed to replace the original booster of the SA-3's V.601 missiles, with boosters taken from old V-755 and V-759 missiles of the SA-2 SAM system. This resulted in an improvement in maximum range from 25,000 to 30,000 metres and an increase in the missile's speed to 50 metres per second.

Both efforts proved highly effective, and eventually a total of 250 V.601 missiles were modified with boosters from V-755 and V-759s, while 24 launchers and other equipment of brigades operating SA-3 systems were installed on a total of 120 Iveco trucks.

US and British fliers underway over Iraq began encountering modified SA-3s in mid-1999 and were initially taken by surprise. During one of the first of resulting engagements, over the northern NFZ, a General Dynamics/Lockheed-Martin F-16C of the US Air Force was narrowly missed by a visually guided V.601 missile, fired by Missile Brigade 232. The weapon was detonated by proximity fuse close enough to the target to cause the jet to start emitting black smoke: nevertheless, the F-16 managed to limp back to Turkey for a safe emergency landing. Meanwhile, the US wingman counterattacked the launcher and scored a direct hit, killing its crew of three, a guard standing nearby, and injuring seven.

Meanwhile, Colonel Hamza was appointed Director of the Air Weapons Directorate and, in 2000–2001, he initiated a project to develop an electronic countermeasures system against the Grumman E-2C Hawkeye AEW aircraft of the US Navy. Led by Brigadier Sinan, who had served with the signals intelligence Unit 128 and was experienced in eavesdropping on US and British military communication before being assigned to the al-Salam Works at Camp Taji, the project resulted in the development of an ECM system that was mobilised through installation on a vehicle, and proved effective in 2001–2002, severely curbing operations of E-2Cs over Iraq. The system in question, the designation of which remains unknown, proved ineffective against the more powerful radar of the Boeing E-3 Sentry though.

ELECTRONIC WARFARE

As described above, Iraq gradually developed a potent electronic warfare capability during the conflict with Iran. That said, it never encountered a massive deployment of anti-radiation missiles as the Iranians had none. Thus, the war of 1991 – during which the US and allied forces deployed about 1,651 AGM-88 HARM (High-speed Anti-Radiation Missile), and over 200 older AGM-45 Shrike – came as an unpleasant surprise and heavily damaged a number of air defence units. The only part of the IrAF-controlled SAM force that avoided this experience were a few S-125/SA-3 units equipped with decoy transmitters that mimicked emissions from their S-125 fire-control radars (ASCC/NATO codename 'Low Blow').

Work on expanding such a capability was relaunched following a series of clashes with US and British airpower in late 1992 and early 1993, and resulted in the series production of decoy fire-control radars. By 1997, a total of 13 such systems were in service, all capable of faking the emissions of not only the S-125's fire-control radar, but also those of the S-75/SA-2's SNR-75 ('Fan Song'), and 2K12/SA-6's 1S91 SURN ('Straight Flush'). While manufacturing these decoys, the Iraqis took great care for these to not only have the same electronic footprint and radar echo, but also the same thermal signature. The project proved its worth during Operation Desert Fox in December 1998, US forces fired more than 100 AGM-88s, of which 66 reportedly scored hits. As far as Iraqi experiences go, this was quite a precise figure – with one substantial difference: of these 66 HARMs, 64 hit decoys, and only two actual operational equipment. Unsurprisingly, the IrAF suffered no losses in personnel during that campaign.

In the light of this success, the Iraqis further intensified their efforts and manufactured about a dozen additional decoys by 2003: As far as is known, nearly all were hit by several missiles (according to the Iraqis, between 1991 and 2003 the US and allied forces deployed 2,284 anti-radiation missiles against Iraq), indicating they had achieved a high degree of effectiveness.

UNMANNED AERIAL VEHICLES

Largely ignored in the West, between the late 1980s and the early 2000s, Iraq carried out the development of several small unmanned aerial vehicles (UAVs, or 'drones'), along with two larger types, which reached flight testing. Initiated in 1987–1988, the first projects aimed to develop small UAVs for surveillance and reconnaissance purposes but did not get very far. In November 1991 – around the same time the air force also flight tested a Mirage F.1EQ equipped with the oversized Irakien drop tank of French origin modified to spray chemicals – the MIC and the IrAF initiated work on converting a disused MiG-21PFM interceptor to a remotely piloted vehicle. The aircraft was equipped with a remote control system acquired from the German company Groupner, an autopilot taken from a MiG-23 fighter-bomber (because this provided a more stable flight and was easier to adapt to its new task), and servo actuators that controlled the throttle, control surfaces, and brakes. The sole flight test was carried out on 10 January 1992 from Rashid Air Base in Baghdad but ended before long: the aircraft almost flipped out of control and the pilot who was in the cockpit was forced to take control of the aircraft and make an emergency landing. Lacking time and expertise to improve the steering system, the project was abandoned.

The work on UAVs was resumed only in 1995, when Huwaysh – who was highly enthusiastic about such aircraft – took over from Husein Kamil and established the Drone Directorate at the MIMI. This time, the development was pursued through two simultaneous projects. The bigger one, led by Dr. Mahmoud Modhaffer, envisaged the conversion of old Aero L-29 Delfin jet trainers into remotely piloted aircraft by the Ibn Firnas Centre, headed by Major General Ibrahim Ismail Smain. As in the case of the MiG-21 four years before, a single L-29 was equipped with a remote control system of German origin (this was connected to the control system of the Italian-made Mirach-100 target UAVs), an autopilot, and four cameras. However, following successful ground testing, the entire project was moved from Rashid AB to al-Mutassim AB, outside Samarra. The first successful test flight was undertaken on 13 April 1997: it was not only successful but was followed by a second successful test flight in June. Therefore, the Iraqis decided to test the system to the maximum range of its command and video signals. In August of the same year, the modified L-29 flew about 60–70km southeast of Mutasim AB when the ground station lost connection and the jet crashed. Ibn Firnas then attempted to improve the controllability through the installation of the stabiliser system from a Chinese-made anti-ship missile and conduct another 21 test flights – interrupted only by the bombing of Mutasim AB during Operation Desert Fox in December 1998. However, when the L-29 was tested for the first time without a pilot in the cockpit in spring 2001, it crashed, leading to the cancellation of the project.

The other effort to obtain UAVs was carried out on Saddam's order by a team of the Military Research and Development Committee led by Dr. Imad Abd al-Latif ar-Rida, as Project Yamamah, starting in 1993. It envisaged the development of several different types of small, custom-designed aircraft, named sequentially from Yamamah 1 to Yamamah 11. Most of these, like Yamamah 2 and Yamamah 4, for example, were propeller driven, and one, Yamamah 3, was jet powered, while Yamamah 11 was used for training purposes. Eventually, the Ibn Firnas Centre focused on the development of propeller-driven UAVs, because they proved much easier to control. Many prototypes came into being, several of which were gradually developed so far that, for example, Yamamah 2 – after its control surfaces and fuel tank were enlarged, and it received a GPS-supported control system – went into production as the Musayara-20 (or 'UAV-20'). In June 2002, this is known to have flown for three hours over a distance of 500km – most of this on autopilot. Unsurprisingly, the Musayara-20 was selected for production and the Republican Guards Forces Command placed an order for 36.

Meanwhile, in early 2000, another, more ambitious project for an armed UAV and a UAV capable of serving as a platform for electronic warfare was launched under the designation al-Qods. Led by Dr. Imad Abd al-Latif ar-Rida, the al-Qods is known to have undergone flight testing, and to have met all the requirements in terms of range, payload, and programmable autonomous guidance, but came into being too late to enter series production before March 2003.

THE LAST CRY

In response to the terrorist attacks of 9/11, Saddam made a particularly bad error in several of his statements that sympathised with the terrorists, in turn enabling the administration of US President George W Bush Junior to align him with the 'Axis of Evil'. In late 2002, Iraq thus came under severe pressure from the international community to enable UN inspectors to return. Too late, Baghdad accepted UN Security Council Resolution 1441 and invited inspectors back to the country, and presented them with its Currently Accurate, Full, and Complete Declaration papers: while mostly containing old information, these did provide details on the Samoud II and Fath projects, and on a number of rebuilt facilities. Concluding that the Samoud II violated Resolution 687, the inspectors stopped the work on flight testing of that project and in March 2003 began supervising the destruction of 72 missiles and three launchers. In similar fashion, the UN inspectors ordered an end of all flight tests of the Fath missiles until they could evaluate its capabilities. However, by that time, the USA and its allies were on the verge of invading the country, and the UN personnel left the country before this task could be completed. The SSMD was thus left with about 30 intact

Samoud IIs and about 20 Faths. As far is known, five Samoud IIs were fired during the following war, before operations were stopped because of continuous malfunctions. Fath performed much better and between 12 and 16 were fired with some success.

Al-Samoud II missile, as found hidden in Amarah, in south-eastern Iraq. (US DoD)

By 2003, Iraqis were making extensive use of commercial trailers to make some of their SAMs mobile, but also to transport spare missiles. This trailer with two Ababil-100/Faths was found somewhere north of Basrah. (US Marine Corps Photo)

Table 8: Known Iraqi Missile Attacks on the US-led Coalition, 2003[1]

Date	Local Time	Missile	Target	Notes
20 March	0942 hrs	Fath	TF Thunder	HQ 101st Airborne Assault Division; first detected by USS *Higgins* off the coast of Kuwait; 3 PAC-2/3 fired
20 March	1030 hrs	Fath	Doha	shot down by PAC-3
20 March	2130 hrs	Fath	unknown	no damage, crashed into the sea
20 March	2208 hrs	Samoud II	unknown	no damage, crashed into the western desert of Kuwait
20 March	2320 hrs	Fath	Udairi	shot down by PAC-2
21 March	1001 hrs	Fath	TF Fox/al-Jahra	shot down by Kuwaiti PAC-2
23 March	unknown	Samoud II	unknown	shot down by PAC-2
24 March	1035 hrs	Samoud II	unknown	shot down by PAC-2
24 March	1342 hrs	Fath	unknown	no damage, crashed into the western desert of Kuwait
25 March	1248 hrs	Fath	unknown	shot down by Kuwaiti PAC-2
26 March	1658 hrs	Fath	unknown	blew up shortly after launch
27 March	0831 hrs	Fath	Doha	shot down by Kuwaiti PAC-2 but debris fell over the Camp Doha
27 March	2056 hrs	Fath	unknown	launched against a target inside Iraq, malfunctioned and crashed in the desert
28 March	2250 hrs	Faw-150	Kuwait City	hit a pier in Kuwait City, killing two civilians
29 March	1500 hrs	Laith	unknown	no damage, crashed in northern Kuwait
1 Apr	0603 hrs	Samoud II	unknown	shot down by PAC-3
1 Apr	unknown	Laith	unknown	no damage
1 Apr	unknown	3x Faw-150	Kuwait City	no damage, all crashed near the border between Iraq and Kuwait
3 Apr	0020 hrs	Laith	Najaf	no damage
3 Apr	0150 hrs	Laith	Najaf	no damage
3 Apr	0152 hrs	Laith	Najaf	no damage
7 Apr	unknown	Fath	Baghdad	hit the HQ 2nd Brigade, 3rd Infantry Division, killing 5, injuring 14

On 19 March 2003, following a build-up over many months, Iraq found itself invaded by a US-led Coalition including the United Kingdom, Australia, and Poland. By that time, the Iraqi armed forces were much weakened, in a generally poor state, suffering from poor morale, and thus largely proved ineffective. The invaders took nothing for granted, though, and thus one of the opening blows included a mission by the British 22nd Special Air Service Regiment (Task Force 14) against a suspected chemical munitions site at a water treatment plant in the town of al-Qaim, in the area from which numerous al-Husseins were fired at Israel in 1991. The 60 members of D Squadron were flown to Iraq in six Boeing MH-47D Chinook helicopters, in three waves, while B Squadron drove overland from Jordan. The approach to the plant was compromised and a firefight developed in which the British lost one vehicle. Unimpressed, the now diminutive SSMD – reduced to the downsized Brigades 225 and 226 – went into action on 20 March, firing its Faths (which became better known amongst Coalition troops as the Ababil-100), Samoud IIs, Faw-150s, and – later on – Laith missiles. Initial operations took place from pre-selected sites south and west of Basra and were reasonably precise considering the almost complete lack of targeting intelligence. Nevertheless, all those threatening Coalition troops were shot down by PAC-2 and PAC-3 Patriot SAMs as, due to experience from 1991, the US and Kuwaiti air defences were significantly improved. The rapid advance of US and British troops eventually forced the SSMD

A pair of Laith-90 missiles captured in 2003. The Iraqis fired at least five during the US invasion of 2003. (US DoD)

US Army troops inspecting the wreckage on the scene of the Ababil-100 strike from 7 April 2003. (US DoD)

Iraq and Kuwait, while one hit an area that had been occupied by units of the I Marine Expeditionary Force a few days before. After this, the remaining TELs were withdrawn to the Hillah area, outside Baghdad, and then to the area south of Kirkuk. This is from where the last few launches of Laith missiles were undertaken on 3 April 2003. Two days later, the first troops of the US Army entered Baghdad, followed by the US Marines. The SSMD still had at least one modified LRSV-262 launcher in operational condition though, and on 7 April 2002 it fired a single Fath from the Hillah area at the headquarters of the 2nd Brigade, 3rd Infantry Division. Because the weapon approached the target from the south, it was not intercepted by PAC SAMs of the US Army. Moreover, the targeting intelligence was much better than usual, and thus the missile scored an almost direct hit. It not only killed three soldiers and two foreign reporters, and injured 14 others, but demolished 22 military vehicles. Ironically, just as in 1991, it was thus the last Iraqi ballistic missile fired in this war that caused the heaviest casualties to the enemy. By 12 April, the capital of Iraq was under US control, followed by Tikrit three days later. On 1 May 2003, US President George W Bush declared an 'end of major combat operations'. During the following days and weeks, the US troops collected about 12 intact Faths and Samoud IIs from various hideouts in southern Iraq. With this, the era of Iraqi research and development of indigenous weapons, and deploying these in combat, came to an end.

to withdraw into new positions in the Najaf and Karbala area by 23 March, which in turn significantly reduced the precision of its strikes. Moreover, by this time Coalition troops had learned to recognise pending attacks very early as the Iraqis always had to release weather balloons to determine weather conditions at different the atmospheric levels.

By 27 March, most of the operational TELs were withdrawn all the way to the Kirkuk area, from where they attempted to target advancing enemy units in southern Iraq. Instead, the units operating Faw-150s went into action by targeting Kuwait City. The first attack achieved surprise and hit a pier outside the Kuwaiti capital, killing two people. As a result, not only did Kuwait partially redeploy its PAC-2 SAM sites, but the Royal Navy positioned the guided-missile destroyer HMS *York* in shallow waters off Kuwait City tasked to intercept Iraqi cruise missiles with its GWS.30 Sea Dart SAM system.

The three Faw-150s launched on 1 April all missed their targets widely: two crashed in the empty desert along the border between

BIBLIOGRAPHY

PRIMARY DOCUMENTS

32nd AAMDC, 'Operation Iraqi Freedom: 32nd Army Air and Missile Defense Command's History of the Patriot in Iraq' (32nd Army Air and Missile Defence Command, PowerPoint presentation)

Brigadier General Ahmad Sadik Rushdie al-Astrabadi, Electronic Warfare of Iraq (unpublished manuscript)

CIA, *Iraq's Air Force: Improving Capabilities, Ineffective Strategy; An Intelligence Assessment*, October 1987, CIA/FOIA/ERR

Comprehensive Report of the Special Advisor to the DCI on Iraq's WMD With Addendums (US Government Office, September 2004)

DIA, *Electronic Warfare Forces Study – Iraq*, 9 August 1990, National Archives

PUBLISHED SOURCES

Alnasrawi, A., *The Economy of Iraq: Oil, Wars, Destruction of Development and Prospects, 1950–2010* (Westport: Greenwood Press, 1994)

Ayyoubi, al-Abd R, '43 Missiles on the Zionist Entity' (in Arabic), *al-Arab al-Yawm*, 1998

Bermudez Jr., J. S., 'Iraqi Missile Operations During "Desert Storm"', *Jane's Soviet Intelligence Review*, Vol. 3, No. 3 (March 1991)

Bermudez Jr., J. S., 'Feedback – Iraq', *Jane's Soviet Intelligence Review*, Vol.2, No. 7 (July 1990)

Cooper, T., *MiG-23 Flogger in the Middle East: Mikoyan i Gurevich MiG-23 in Service in Algeria, Egypt, Iraq, Libya and Syria, 1973–2018* (Warwick: Helion & Co., 2018)

Cooper, T., Sadik, *Général de Brigade* A., Bishop, F., *La guerre Iran-Irak: Les combat aériens, Hors-Serie Avions No. 22 & No. 23* (Outreau: Éditions LELA PRESSE, 2007)

Cooper, T., Sipos, M., *Iraqi Mirages: The Dassault Mirage Family in Service with the Iraqi Air Force, 1981–1988* (Warwick: Helion & Co., 2018)

Cooper, T., Sipos, M., *Wings of Iraq, Volume 2: The Iraqi Air Force, 1970–1980* (Warwick: Helion & Co., 2021)

Hiro, D., *The Longest War: The Iran–Iraq Military Conflict* (Oxon: Routledge, Chapman and Hall Inc., 1991)

Hooton, E. R., Cooper, T., Nadimi, F., *The Iran–Iraq War, Volume 1: The Battle for Khuzestan, September 1980–May 1982* (Solihull: Helion & Co Ltd, 2016)

Hooton, E. R., Cooper, T., Nadimi, F., *The Iran–Iraq War, Volume 2: Iran Strikes Back, June 1982–December 1986* (Solihull: Helion & Co Ltd, 2016)

Hooton, E. R., Cooper, T., Nadimi, F., *The Iran–Iraq War, Volume 3: Iraq's Triumph* (Solihull: Helion & Co Ltd, 2017)

Hooton, E. R., Cooper, T., Nadimi, F., *The Iran–Iraq War, Volume 4: The Forgotten Fronts* (Solihull: Helion & Co Ltd, 2017)

Hooton, E. R. & Cooper, T., *Desert Storm, Volume 1: The Iraqi Invasion of Kuwait and Operation Desert Shield, 1990–1991* (Warwick: Helion & Co., 2019)

Hoyt, T. D., *Military Industry and Regional Defense Policy; India, Iraq and Israel* (Oxon: Routledge, 2007)

Hybel, A. R., Kaufman, J. M., *The Bush Administration and Saddam Hussein: Deciding on the Conflict* (Palgrave Macmillan, 2006).

Lennox, D., 'Iraq's Short Range Surface-to-Surface Missiles', *Jane's Soviet Intelligence Review*, Vol. 3, No. 2 (February 1991)

Lennox, D. (editor), *Jane's Air-Launched Weapons* (Surrey: Jane's Information Group Ltd., 2001)

Lewis, G. N., Fetter, S., Gronlund, L., *Casualties and Damage from Scud Attacks in the 1991 Gulf War* (Boston: MIT, DACS Working Paper, 1993)

Liébert, M. & Buyck, S., *Le Mirage F1 et les Mirage de seconde generation à voilure en flèche, Vol.1* (Outreau: Éditions LELA PRESSE, 2007)

Lowther, W., *Iraq and the Supergun: Gerald Bull, the true Story of Saddam Hussein's Dr Doom* (London: Pan Books Ltd., 1992)

Richardson, D., *Techniques and Equipment of Electronic Warfare* (London: Salamander Books Ltd., 1985)

Rostker, B. (editor), *Information Paper: Iraq's Scud Ballistic Missiles* (nuke.fas.org, last update 25 July 2000)

Sadik, Brig Gen A. & Cooper, T., 'Les "Mirage" de Baghdad: les Dassault "Mirage" F1 dans la force aérienne irakienne', *Fana de l'Aviation No. 434/2006*; 'Deuxième partie', *Fana de l'Aviation No. 435/2006*

Sadik, Brig Gen A. & Cooper, T., 'Un Falcon 50 lance-missiles: Avion d'affaires contre navire de guerre', *Fana de l'Aviation No. 470* (2007)

Sadik, Brig Gen A., and Cooper, T. *Iraqi Fighters, 1953–2003: Camouflage & Markings* (Houston: Harpia Publishing, 2008)

Sampson, A., *Die Waffenhändler: Von Krupp bis Lockheed, Die Geschichte eines tödlichen Geschäfts* (Reinbek bei Hamburg: Rowohl Verlag GmbH, 1977)

Seth Carus, W & Bermudez Jr., J. S., 'Iraq's al-Husayn Missile Programme'; *Jane's Soviet Intelligence Review*, Vol. 2, No. 5 (May 1990)

Seth Carus, W. & Bermudez Jr., J. S., 'Iraq's al-Husayn Missile Programme', *Jane's Soviet Intelligence Review*, Vol. 2, No. 6 (June 1990)

Shakibania, M. & Bibak, S., *Tomcat Fights* (TV documentary, Iran, 2012)

Shaw, I., and Santana, S., *Beyond the Horizon: The History of AEW&C Aircraft* (Houston: Harpia Publishing LLC, 2014)

Sipos, M., Cooper, T., *Wings of Iraq, Volume 2: The Iraqi Air Force, 1970-1980* (Warwick, Helion & Co., 2021)

NOTES

CHAPTER 1

1   Sadik, interview, 10/2007.

CHAPTER 2

1   The MiG-25 could, in theory, reach a maximum speed of more than Mach 3. However, this capability was rarely used because the engines tended to overspeed and were then damaged beyond repair as a consequence. Therefore, pilots would accelerate this fast only in the event that this was absolutely necessary.

2   For details on the deployment of R-17Es during the opening Iraqi strike on Iranian air bases, see Cooper et al, *Wings of Iraq, Volume 2*.

CHAPTER 3

1   Unless stated otherwise, this chapter is based on Cooper et al, *Iraqi Mirages*.

2   J. H., retired missile warfare analyst of the DIA, interview, 10/2002.

3   Sadik, interviews with Tom Cooper, 03/2007 & 10/2007; Sadik et al, *La guerre Iran-Irak, No.23*; and Cooper et al, *Iraqi Mirages*.

CHAPTER 4

1   All three factories involved in the production of the CB-250K were heavily bombed and destroyed during the war in 1991.

2   Notably, the US Army never used the MGM-designation for the Pershing II; only for the Pershing I.

CHAPTER 5

1   Cooper et al, *Wings of Iraq, Volume 2*; O'Ballance, pp.73–74 & 102–103; Alfredo André, interview, September 2018.

2   Alfredo André, interview, September 2018 & Hoyt.

3   Alfredo André, interview, September 2018.

4   Reportedly, Kuwait followed in fashion and placed an order for 24 firing units and 24,000 R-262 rockets. Of course, this order was never fulfilled.

CHAPTER 6

1   Lowther, pp.15–100.

2   Lowther, pp.100–102.

3   Sadik, interviews, 03/2005, 03/2006 & 03/2007. Before long, the Iraqis were placing sufficient orders for EXPAL-made BR.250 and BR.500 general purpose bombs, for the Spaniards to establish a new company – International Technology SA – tasked with 'further development of designs based on the Mk.80 series, new domestic designs, and associated air-driven fuses' (Lennox, *Jane's Air-Launched Weapons*, pp.450–455). According to the leading Portuguese military aviation researcher, Jose Augusto Matos (interview, 12/2018), related Portuguese documentation remains beyond public reach at present, but it seems that the Portuguese company COMETNA (a national metallurgical company supervised by the Ministry of Industry and Technology) was occasionally contracted by either Baghdad or EXPAL for the production of casings for aviation bombs: these would then be forwarded to the Trafaria Explosives Factory (in Portugal), which added their explosive content. The resulting production was undertaken only in response to sporadic requests, i.e. it was anything but 'continuous' (a fact important because at least officially, the production of aviation bombs in Portugal ceased once

the country withdrew from its overseas possessions in 1975, and was relaunched only once the EMPORDEF Group was established in 1997).

CHAPTER 7

NONE

CHAPTER 8

1   DIA, *EWFS-Iraq*, pp.iii & 12.

2   Sadik, interviews, 03/2005, 03/2006, 03/2007; 10/2007; Shakibania et al, *Tomcat Fights*; Hooton et al, *Iran–Iraq War, Vol.3*, pp.20–21; Iraqi Air Force Martyrs Website & Cooper et al, *Iraqi Mirages*.

3   DIA, *EWFS-Iraq*, p.10, CIA/FOIA/ERR.

4   Indeed, as subsequently reported by Bermudez et al in 'Iraq's al-Husayn Missile Programe', Baghdad then announced the existence of the new missile, on 3 August 1987, and claimed it flew a distance of 615km.

5   Seth Carus et al, Iraq's al-Husayn Missile Programe', *Jane's Soviet Intelligence Review*, Vol.2, No. 6 (June 1990), pp.242–248.

CHAPTER 9

1   S/1999/94, 'Letter dated 27 January 1999 from the Permanent Representatives of the Netherlands and Slovenia to the United Nations, Addressed to the President of the Security Council', 27 January 1999, *United Nations* (un.org)

2   Fate had it that, after leaving all three ex-Iraqi jets to decay for more than a decade 'in open storage', the Iranians reactivated one of the Adnan-1s, renamed it *Simorgh*, applied the serial number 5-8208, and attempted to fly it on a parade over Tehran, on 22 September 2009. The unavailing catastrophe occurred minutes before the jet reached the Iranian capital: the radome detached and hit the fin, causing a loss of control: the aircraft crashed near Varmin with the loss of all seven crewmembers.

3   Sadik, interview, October 2007.

CHAPTER 10

1   Unless stated otherwise, based on Lowther, pp.186–190.

2   S/1999/94, 'Letter dated 27 January 1999 from the Permanent Representatives of the Netherlands and Slovenia to the United Nations, Addressed to the President of the Security Council', 27 January 1999, *United Nations* (un.org)

3   For the latter thesis, see Hybel et al, *The Bush Administration and Saddam Hussein*.

CHAPTER 11

1   Unless stated otherwise, based Hooton et al, *Desert Storm*, Volume 1., pp.18, 28–29 & S/1999/94, 'Letter dated 27 January 1999 from the Permanent Representatives of the Netherlands and Slovenia to the United Nations, Addressed to the President of the Security Council', 27 January 1999, *United Nations* (un.org)

2   S/1999/94, 'Letter dated 27 January 1999 from the Permanent Representatives of the Netherlands and Slovenia to the United Nations, Addressed to the President of the Security Council', 27 January 1999, *United Nations* (un.org)

3   S/1999/94, 'Letter dated 27 January 1999 from the Permanent Representatives of the Netherlands and Slovenia to the United Nations, Addressed to the President of the Security Council', 27 January 1999, *United Nations* (un.org)

4   Based on Cooper, *MiG-23 in the Middle East*.

5   Based on Cooper, *In the Claws of the Tomcat*.

6   '92 Senegal Soldiers Killed in Saudi Arabia Air Crash', *The New York Times*, 22 March 1991.

7   Ayyubi, *43 Missiles on the Zionist Entity*.

8   S/1999/94, 'Letter dated 27 January 1999 from the Permanent Representatives of the Netherlands and Slovenia to the United Nations, Addressed to the President of the Security Council', 27 January 1999, *United Nations* (un.org)

CHAPTER 12

1   Based on 'Operation Iraqi Freedom: 32nd Army Air and Missile Defense Command', pp.47–83.